I Want a Teaching Job !

Guide to Getting the Teaching Job of Your Dreams

Tim Wei

Wei, Tim

Title: I Want a Teaching Job:

           Guide to Getting the Teaching Job of Your Dreams / Tim Wei

ISBN: 1-450-53796-0

EAN 13:   978-1450537964

Published by TPW Websites

Book cover character by Luvlee Design

Book cover design by Caius V.

Internal graphics by royalty-free subscription from Clipart.com

Edited by Cynthia Sherwood

Table of Contents

Guide to Getting the Teaching Job of Your Dreams

- Chapter 1 -

So You Want a Teaching Job?

You've finished college. You're done with your student teaching. Maybe you've even been a substitute teacher for a while. Now you want to get a continuing contract as a full-time teacher. You've come to the right place.

The *Guide to Getting the Teaching Job of Your Dreams* will walk you through the increasingly competitive process of hunting for teaching jobs. Gone are the days when you could submit your paperwork and wait for the phone to ring. Today's job search requires a detailed marketing plan. My goal for this book is to give you down-to-earth, simple advice for finding the perfect, career-level teaching job.

If you've searched on the Internet for information about teaching jobs, you've probably noticed that real, solid, in-depth advice is hard to come by. You may find a few "sample interview questions," some general advice about how to act at an interview, and some brief tips from teachers on forums. While you can find helpful people and resources on-line, I've found that the vast majority of information is written by people who have had no personal experience interviewing for teaching jobs.

Who am I and why am I writing this book? Simply put, I am an experienced teacher who has been to the interview table several times as a candidate and many more times as an interviewer. I've worked for two different school districts, and I've taught over 900 elementary-aged students. I'm an experienced educator, an experienced teacher interviewer, and experienced teacher interviewee.

I share my personal knowledge, experience, and insight into the teacher job hunting process because I am all too familiar with the agony that goes into selling yourself. So that you can avoid some of the frustration and hardship that I and countless others have experienced during the job search process, I am writing this guide to help **you** win the teaching job you want. I'm not a hobbyist who writes books on a wide variety of topics to get rich quick, so I have a narrow focus that applies specifically to your situation.

By the time they've finished student teaching, most graduates are extremely anxious to embark on their new teaching career. They're full of fresh ideas, motivated to share their knowledge with kids, and ready to work hard. If you're beginning this new stage of your career, I'm sure you're excited to face the challenges ahead.

Anyone who says it's easy to find a teaching job because there are severe teacher shortages across the country is probably unfamiliar with the realities of education today. While the job market does vary from place to place, most American cities have a surplus of qualified teachers. At my school, it's not uncommon to have 200 or more applications for a single job opening! Unfortunately, this means most candidates— even the most highly qualified ones— will have a long, challenging job hunt ahead of them.

With patience, preparation, a little luck, lots of hard work, and some creative marketing strategies, you can make yourself stand out as a top candidate in the best schools. If you simply read the help wanted ads, send in a few applications, and wait by the phone, you may be waiting a long time. You'll need to take further action to get noticed. You'll need to improve your résumé, write powerful cover letters, call Human Resource offices, walk in to meet principals, assemble an impressive teaching portfolio, and practice sample interview questions.

But is it worth it? Why would someone spend months and months of their time doing all this work– for a job that seems impossible to get? I mean, all you want to do is teach! You just want to get in a classroom and share knowledge with children! You already know the rewards of teaching! You know how exciting it is when a student's face lights up because he/she "finally gets it." You know the joys of being responsible for a child's academic and emotional growth. And you know that each student is unique and will influence your life in a positive way. But how do you break into such a rewarding career when the odds seem to be stacked against you?

You **can** land a job in even the most saturated markets. There will always be *some* openings in almost every school— even the best-paying ones and sought-after suburban schools. There will be retirements, teachers taking extended leave to spend time with their families, and changes in enrollment. It's not uncommon for even the best school districts to have openings every single year.

All you have to do to land one of these jobs is **prove** how much you love working with students, **show** that you're one of the most dedicated and caring teachers available, and **prepare** yourself to take the job market by storm. Many will try to find a job each year, but only a few will be successful. The best jobs will go to the candidates who are the most qualified and put forth the greatest effort in their job search.

Unlike the temporary, unskilled jobs you may have had during high school and college, chances are you will probably keep your job as a teacher until you retire. You will work with the same people day in and day out for the next few decades of your life. This is why it is essential to begin your job search by determining what type of environment you want to work in.

Exactly what kind of job would you like?

Answer the questions below. Be honest with yourself. Remember, your choices shouldn't be based on what other people think you should do. You should decide what you feel is best for yourself.

1. Do you want to work in an inner-city school, a suburban school, or a rural school?

2. Would you prefer a public school, a private school, or a religious school?

3. Would you be more comfortable in a large school or a small school?

4. Do you want to remain in your community, or would you prefer to move to a new place?

5. What grade levels are you qualified to work with? What grade levels would you prefer?

6. Are you open to being a substitute teacher or a teacher's aide before you begin teaching as a "regular" teacher?

7. What can you absolutely *not* tolerate in a school? What would you *love* to see in a school?

Since you probably don't want to repeat the job search process in a few years, you should do everything in your power to get a job at the schools where you would most like to work.

Don't settle for a job you won't truly enjoy. Your job will be more than a job; it will be a lifestyle that determines how your days are spent. You'll want to work in a place with positive administrators, teachers, and students who are compatible with your teaching style and abilities.

Many teachers quit their jobs within their first few years of teaching. They become stressed and burned-out. Sometimes student discipline becomes too much of a burden. Sometimes the workload is too excessive. Sometimes teachers aren't passionate about the subjects they're required to teach. When this happens, people think they're not meant to be teachers. More often than not, it's not teaching that burns people out, it's the school or the job itself.

If you teach a subject you enjoy, at a school you love, with colleagues and students that make your day brighter, you won't become stressed and your teaching career will be just as fulfilling as you imagined it to be.

This is not a book to find shortcuts and secrets. There is no "quick and easy" way to earn the perfect teaching job. Rather, this book is an in-depth guide to the job hunting process. It's meant to give you advice and information on the many challenging steps you'll have to take to secure a teaching job.

If you put in a little extra effort to find and win the job that's right for you, you will never doubt the choices you've made.

- Chapter 2 -

The Best Places to Start Searching for Your Perfect Job

Once you've earned your teaching certification, it's time to find a school that is in need of teachers. Of course, depending on your geographic area, the amount of competition in the job market will vary.

Where are all the jobs?

These days, teacher shortages in the United States are relatively uncommon. However, some states and cities simply have more job openings than others. Your job search will be much less difficult if you look for jobs in places with a growing population, a booming economy, and high quality-of-life.

Schools will be growing and doing more hiring in places with bustling populations of young families. Look for places where new housing is popping up, business and commercial districts are growing, and schools are expanding.

Where is it tough to find a job?

Some cities have dozens—even hundreds—of candidates for each available position. Cities with competitive teaching job markets often have a shrinking population, high taxes, and/or low economic growth. Also, cities with several large teaching colleges nearby tend to have an overflow of qualified candidates.

But remember, just because a city has a competitive job market doesn't mean you won't get a job. You will just have to work harder to find the job that's right for you. Every school needs to hire new teachers sometime. Candidates need to market themselves more aggressively and put more effort into their job search.

Examples of places that have the largest overflow of qualified teachers include Michigan, Upstate New York, Pennsylvania, Ohio, and New Jersey. Due to sharp budget cuts in education, jobs are becoming increasingly difficult to find in states like California and Florida as well.

Also, communities that have many teacher colleges tend to have much more competitive job markets. You may want to look for regions where there aren't as many graduates leaving college with teaching degrees.

Before You Hop on a Plane....

If you do have the freedom and the desire to move, be sure you do your research. Don't just hop on a plane to the city with the most available teaching jobs.

You're looking for a teaching job **and** a place that feels like home. Choosing where to teach shouldn't be based on job availability alone. You deserve to live an enjoyable lifestyle. You don't want to get the perfect job in a city you're really not happy with.

Be sure to find out how much the community values their schools. Determine:

1. How well teachers are paid
2. How big the class sizes are
3. How many days are in a school year
4. How much standardized testing the state requires
5. Whether or not you'll need a Master's degree to teach
6. How the area rates in terms of student achievement

If you're considering a move to a new city, don't forget to research non-school-related issues, such as:

1. Cost of Living
2. Taxes
3. Climate
4. Quality of Life

Okay, I Know Where I Want to Live! Now How Do I Find a Job?

Unfortunately, in most areas, the market is over-saturated with candidates. This means you'll have to spend more time and put more effort into your job search. If this is the case for you, where do you begin?

Searching for Jobs on the Internet

One of the first places many people begin to search for a teaching job is the Internet. Try to target job sites that are specifically designed for teachers.

Among the best-known sites for teachers jobs are:

> ABCTeachingJobs - www.abcteachingjobs.com
>
> SchoolSpring - www.schoolspring.com
>
> TeacherJobs.com - www.teacherjobs.com
>
> Teachers.net - jobs.teachers.net
>
> Teachers-Teachers - www.teachers-teachers.com

These sites all offer free membership for teacher candidates to search for jobs, though some of them offer enhanced services for an extra fee.

Most teacher job sites will allow you to upload your résumé and cover letter, and you can search through thousands of available positions across the country and around the world.

Many even have on-line portfolio features that allow you to submit your application automatically to districts that you choose.

The largest job and most widely used job search site for teachers is SchoolSpring.com. Many teachers I've talked with have had positive experiences using it. They've said it's easy to use and comprehensive. If you're using the Internet to look for jobs, you may want to start here.

Because they seem to be the most popular job search site for teachers, I wanted to go into a little more depth in describing the features of SchoolSpring. Many of these features are available on other sites as well.

SchoolSpring On-line Job Search Tips and Tricks

SchoolSpring Search Agent

Create a "search agent." This allows employers to find you if they're searching the candidate pool. You don't want to wait around for employers to find you, although it does happen from time to time. Unless you absolutely need to hide your information, provide "full access" so they're more likely to find you.

Candidates who take the time to add a personal introduction to their Search Agent tend to be more successful. Also, candidates with introductions appear above those without introductions in the search results.

Be sure to add your certifications in the *My Account* section. Many employers will restrict their search to job seekers who are certified. You don't want to miss out because you failed to enter your certification information.

When adding certifications, make sure the correct job categories are checked off.

Entering Your Résumé into SchoolSpring

Use the Résumé Builder to present your résumé as you would on paper. SchoolSpring allows you to include custom sections and change the order of your résumé sections.

Be sure you proofread your on-line résumé, just as you would your paper copy. Firefox has a built-in spell checker — use it.

Don't paste your entire résumé in an "additional information" résumé section. Take the time to enter your education and experience in the appropriate area and create separate sections for other information, such as Awards and Honors, Memberships, Volunteering, etc. Remember, your SchoolSpring résumé *is* a real résumé. If you rush through it and it looks sloppy, employers will not be impressed.

When you enter your information into a SchoolSpring résumé, you can use basic HTML tags to create bold or italicized text and bulleted or numbered lists. Use these features so your résumé stands out from the others. If you don't know how to use basic HTML tags, do a quick Google search. It will take you about five minutes to learn.

Using SchoolSpring's Advanced Search

Use the advanced search for more detailed searching. Here you'll find a keyword search option that can help you zoom into the jobs that really suit your individual qualifications and desires.

Filling Out SchoolSpring's On-line Job Applications

Be sure to customize your cover letter for each job application. To do this, simply save a cover letter template in "My Account" so that you can easily pull it up and customize it when you apply for a particular position. When employers see a customized cover letter, they'll know you're serious about wanting to work at a particular school over others.

Type and save answers to any application questions in a program like Microsoft Word. Then copy and paste them into the on-line application forms. This will allow you to retain a copy of your answers for future applications.

And Don't Forget to Look Beyond SchoolSpring

SchoolSpring.com is not the only job search site for teachers out there, but it is the largest one I am aware of, and I know of many people who have had positive experiences with it. In addition to the sites mentioned on page 14, you can easily find more by doing a simple Google search for "teaching jobs."

While you're on the computer, you may also want to try searching individual school district websites and looking for an "employment" link. Keep in mind that some school districts are often slow to update their websites. Just because they have no jobs listed on-line, doesn't mean they don't have current openings.

Don't waste your time with sites like Monster.com, CareerBuilder.com, and HotJobs.com. You will find very few, if any, teaching jobs on those sites. The few teaching jobs that are posted are often just part-time tutoring for large companies.

While you may find what you're looking for on the Internet, don't be too disappointed if your searches are fruitless. Remember, many teaching positions are never posted on national job search websites.

Have You Read the Newspaper Classifieds?

Browse the career section of your local paper. Very often, districts that are hiring will post an ad in the "help wanted" section. Schools usually post classified ads when they have advance notice of job openings and are trying to compile a large selection of highly-qualified candidates to choose from.

Attend a Career Fair for Teachers

Many cities have career fairs for teachers. Some people return from career fairs very excited and optimistic because they have new leads for job opportunities. Others are extremely disappointed because they expected more personal attention from recruiters.

If you attend a career fair, dress professionally. Take your teaching portfolio and several copies of your application packet with you. Each application packet should include a generic cover letter, résumé, copy of your certification, copy of your college transcript, and letters of recommendation.

Many career fairs tend to be meet-and-greet situations. You'll meet lots of people and learn lots of information about different school districts. You may walk away with a few applications that you can fill out at home.

Some career fairs will offer on-the-spot interviews. If you do have the opportunity to participate in an interview, it's usually just a ten-minute screening interview. Basically, the interviewer is trying to find out if your application is worth keeping on file. Be prepared to highlight all of your strengths in a very short period of time.

If you give your application packet to an interviewer, don't forget to follow-up on it in a week or so. Call the district from home and ask them if they have all of your necessary paperwork on file.

Use Your Networking Skills

Networking can be one of the most helpful tools of all. Talk to teachers you already know and ask if there are any openings at their school. Oftentimes, they can even put in a good word for you when they chat with their principal.

When it is time to fill a vacancy, principals have many teachers approach them to talk about people that would make good candidates. It seems everyone has a friend or a neighbor or a niece or a nephew or a sister or a brother who is looking for a teaching job. Many principals will listen to the recommendations of their teachers when choosing which candidates to call in for an interview.

It's not uncommon for an administrator to offer an interview as a professional courtesy. If you excel at networking, you might have an extra opportunity to get an interview that you might not have had otherwise.

If you do apply to a school where you already know a teacher, be sure you use him or her as a reference on your application.

And the Number One Way to Find Teaching Jobs...

Better than the newspaper.... Better than jobs fairs.... Better than the Internet.... The BEST source for finding teaching jobs is.... the humble telephone book. Why? Many districts don't advertise at all, especially if the market is saturated with qualified teaching candidates. Very often, they've got a pool of applications in the Human Resources office before a vacancy has even been announced.

The unadvertised positions are the easiest jobs to land because there is less competition. Positions that are advertised heavily in the paper and on websites will have far more candidates applying.

Open the phone book. Look in the section that lists school districts. Call every local district you want to work for and ask if they will be hiring a teacher with your certification requirements. Even when schools don't advertise job openings to the public, they'll still tell you on the phone whether or not they're going to be hiring. If there are openings available, you'll be an applicant while other candidates will still be reading the paper, waiting for that help wanted ad to appear.

If they say they're not hiring at this time, they will probably still ask you to send a résumé and cover letter for them to keep on file. This way, if an opening does come up at the last minute, you'll already be in their bank of potential candidates.

Don't search all over looking for job advertisements. Just get on the phone and ask the schools yourself!

- Chapter 3 -

Application Packet: Documents Schools Need to Receive

Not too long ago, when you applied for a teaching job, you'd be submitting a whole packet of paperwork via snail mail. Today, many schools require candidates to fill out on-line applications. While all districts may not require the same paperwork that was submitted in the past, you MUST still have all of it ready for districts that do, and you'll need printed copies of the documents to send directly to principals (more on that later).

Some districts still require traditional paperwork when you apply. Others may request scanned copies of your documents. It is best to have all documents prepared and ready-to-go before you apply for a single job.

While requirements may vary from place to place, some of the documents usually included in an application packet will be:

- Cover letter
- Résumé
- Application (on-line or written)
- Copy of your teaching certificate
- Copy of your teacher certification test scores
- Official college transcript
- A few letters of recommendation

Save yourself some work. Instead of compiling these application packets individually, make lots of copies and put several packets together at one time. In all likelihood, you'll be applying to many different school districts before you're offered a job. If you have your application packets pre-made and ready to go, you'll save yourself time and frustration.

When sending documents by snail mail, an application packet should be kept flat and placed in a large 9×12 inch envelope. Don't overstuff a legal-sized envelope with paper. When a school district opens the envelope, you want them to have nice, professional-looking documents, not a pile of creased and crinkled papers.

After you've mailed in your paperwork or sent them the required digital files, call the district's Human Resources office to be sure they've received everything they need. Even if you know all of your necessary documents were included in your application packet, call the district anyway. This will force them to bring your file back to the top of the pile, and it might help to keep your name fresh in their minds.

Most districts will tell you to send your documents to the Human Resources office. Don't stop there. Go to the computer and type a nice, professional-looking letter to the principals of the schools you want to work at. In your letter, introduce yourself, give a brief overview of your teaching philosophy, compliment the school, and let the principal know you're interested in a job. Attach a résumé to your letter for the principal to review. You can hand-deliver your principal letter or you can mail it.

> **Be sure <u>School Principals</u> also receive a copy of your résumé.**

Here's why this works: Many HR offices often receive dozens (sometimes hundreds) of applications. When it comes time to hire somebody, the Human Resources office will typically give the principal a pile of applications to look through.

Often the HR office only gives the principal a **few** of the applications. There's a good chance the HR office might not even send your application to the principal at all.

If you send a copy of your paperwork to the principal **and** the HR office, you are guaranteed to have been seen by the person who will actually do the hiring.

Remember: Most of the decision-making is done by the school principal, NOT the Human Resources office. If Human Resources doesn't know your name, it's not going to be a big deal. But you **definitely** want to be sure the principal knows who you are.

In most school districts, principals are able to personally choose and hire candidates. Yes, you should fill out those applications and send all necessary paperwork to district offices. They won't be allowed to hire you if you don't. But be sure you follow up with direct communication with the principals of the schools you would like to work at.

If you remember only one important piece of advice from this e-book, it should be this:

> **Direct communication with school principals is the key to landing a teaching job!**

When to Apply

While jobs can open up at any time, most job openings will start at the beginning of the school year. Most principals don't want to worry about hiring teachers all summer, so they typically begin the hiring process in the spring months.

If you wait until July to submit your application, most schools will have their vacant positions already filled. If you hand them an application in December, your paperwork might be at the back of the filing cabinet, and they might forget all about you by the time hiring comes around. If possible, the ideal time to submit your application is around **March** or **April** unless you know of a specific job that will be open before the end of the year. If you've already missed the deadline, send out your paperwork anyway. Maybe you'll be the lucky recipient of an interview to fill a last-minute opening.

What if you're student teaching and you won't graduate until May? You should still send your application packet to the school in March or April, even if you're not done with your student teaching. Mention in your cover letter that you are student teaching and you will be fully certified by the end of the school year. If possible, send along a letter from your college dean stating that you are expected to graduate. Then, as soon as you graduate, send the district an updated application packet with your current credentials.

As I mentioned in the last chapter, if the Human Resources office tells you that there are no job openings, don't give up. Ask them if you can fill out an application so they can keep it on file. Sometimes they'll find out about a last-minute retirement. Sometimes an unexpected maternity leave creates a vacancy. Sometimes enrollment changes, causing the school to hire one more candidate at the last minute. When these things happen, schools don't have time to advertise. They just take the applications on-hand and set up some quick interviews.

After you've submitted your application, remember to follow up on it. You can call Human Resources on the phone or you could even drop by the office in person. Introduce yourself and ask them if they've received all the necessary paperwork.

- Chapter 4 -

Cover Letters and Résumés: Looking Good on Paper

Your cover letter and résumé will show the school whether you are a true professional or not. Before arranging an interview, they're going to quickly glance through your paperwork to see if you are qualified.

They'll also be noticing how you present yourself on paper. If you articulate your goals, objectives, and teaching philosophy well, the school will know that you are a good communicator with professional writing skills.

The Cover Letter: First Impression

Your cover letter can be addressed either to the Superintendent or to the Human Resources Office (or, if the district has one, the Superintendent of Human Resources).

Make each cover letter unique. Mention the district by name in the body of the letter. Human Resources receives many, many letters and they recognize a form letter when they see one. Show them you put the extra effort in to personalize your cover letter.

You don't need to write a novel. The cover letter only needs to be one page long.

Just tell them what you want (a teaching job), add a short summary of your qualifications, summarize your teaching philosophy in a sentence or two, sprinkle in a few compliments about how great the school is, and say thank you.

Your cover letter should be typed and printed on nice, thick, fancy paper.

Find Someone Who is a Good Proofreader!

Have a friend or family member proofread your cover letter to check for mistakes. Anyone who glances at it for five seconds and says, "It's fine," really didn't proofread carefully enough. Find somebody who will actually look carefully for your mistakes. Believe me, if you misspell a common word or if your grammar is way off, you will not be called in for an interview.

Make Your Cover Letter Stand Out From the Rest!

Principals will be reading through cover letter after cover letter. After a while, they all blend together like a sea of white papers. You need your paper to stand out from the rest so it is not overlooked.

Some ways to make your cover letter stand out:

- Develop a catchy opening sentence
- Use bold print to emphasize important words
- Insert a teaching-related graphic in your heading
- Use a bulleted list in the body of your letter
- Add some color to your letterhead

Keep your layout and appearance professional, but figure out which tricks will make your letter the one that stands out among the other, boring cover letters. The principal or Human Resources director will be flipping through many letters. Your letter should be the one that makes them pause, read, and think. If your cover letter doesn't stand out from the rest, the person reviewing your credentials might overlook your best qualifications, skills, experiences, and your passion for teaching.

Sample Cover Letter

Mary Smith
1234 Beech Road
Youngstown, NY 55512

smith96@aol.com
708-352-7381

Dr. Jane Little, Superintendent
Lewiston School District
123 Main Street
Lewiston, NY 55513

April 2, 2010

Dear Ms. Little,

I was excited to see a new position for a **second grade teacher at Lewiston Elementary School**. I immediately completed the on-line application and would like to share some comments my colleagues have made about me:

> *...a hard-working and dedicated professional who emphasizes student learning as her highest priority.*
>
> - Mark Jones, Principal, Lincoln Park School, Wheatfield, NY

> *...creative curriculum developer...an excellent addition to any staff.*
>
> - Cindy Brown, Second Grade Team Leader, Maple Street School, Kenmore, NY

> *...always comes to work with a smile on her face and ready to teach...a phenomenal asset to any school.*
>
> - Dr. Cara Williams, Daemen College Supervisor

I believe my **lifetime of experience** working with children in a wide variety of settings (including public school classrooms), combined with the knowledge I gained by **graduating with honors** from a rigorous adult studies program, and my **enthusiasm and energy** make me an ideal candidate.

In addition to the professional accomplishments detailed in my résumé, I have always taken a personal interest in student success. Even before I became a certified teacher, I frequently volunteered in activities that enriched the lives of children in my community such as the teaching arts and crafts programs to support the **Cheektowaga Park's Summer Camp** and working for the Homework Helpers Program at the **Amherst Boys' and Girls' Club**.

In any teaching situation my goal is the same: **to help each individual develop and learn to his or her fullest potential.** Thank you so much for your time and consideration. I hope to talk with you soon.

Sincerely,

Mary Smith

cc: Mr. Michael Green, Principal of Lewiston Elementary School

Résumé: Outline of Your Abilities and Achievements

The type of résumé you create will depend on your background. If you're an experienced teacher, you should have a résumé centered on your past teaching jobs. If you're a new teacher, you may want to create a résumé that emphasizes your skills and abilities, as well as your experiences working with kids.

Even if you don't have previous teaching experience, you can still fill a résumé. List your student teaching under the heading "Experiences" just as if they were real jobs. You might want to add a short philosophy statement near the top. If you've worked with kids before (at a day care, summer camp, or wherever), be sure to mention it. If you have the space, you can include your volunteer work.

Many teachers write their teaching certificate type and number on the résumé. This gives the Human Resources office a quick reference to your qualifications.

Work experience that is listed on your résumé should either be a long-term experience or teaching-related experience. They don't need to know you worked at McDonald's for two months when you were in high school. They *would* want to know that you worked as a preschool teacher's assistant for six months while in college. Don't hide or embellish your work history; be sure everything on the résumé is honest and legit.

Instead of listing your references on the résumé, you may just write "References provided upon request." If you're short on space, why waste valuable résumé real estate to write other people's addresses? Your references will be on the application anyway. A résumé is supposed to be about **you**, and it does not have to be cluttered with names and addresses of other people.

> It will take you hours to create the perfect résumé.
>
> It will take them fifteen seconds to review it.

Your résumé should probably take up one page if you're relatively new to the teaching profession, but you may use two pages if you have some experience. If you use three pages, you're listing way too much. If you don't fill a full page, your résumé will appear incomplete. One or two full pages is perfect. If you mess around with the line spacing and margins in Microsoft Word, you can make it happen.

Remember, when you submit your application packet, the principal and/or the people at Human Resources are going to glance at your cover letter and résumé quickly. In the real world, no administrator is going to spend five or ten minutes examining each résumé in detail. In fact, only about fifteen seconds will be spent reviewing any given page.

Look at your own résumé and cover letter. Give yourself about fifteen seconds to read through each. Can you get the "gist" of your documents in that short amount of time? If not, make changes so that your accomplishments and experiences stand out at a glance.

Which Résumé Format Should I Use?

Many books and websites will tell you that there is a single, correct way to write a résumé. This is not true. If you looked through a pile of applicant resumés, you'll find that everyone uses a different format, different paper, and lists slightly different information.

The key to a good résumé is to be sure that you include all of the basic information about your background, education, qualifications, experiences, and abilities. As long as it is easy-to-read, you can use any professional-looking layout.

My advice is to do a Google search for sample teaching résumés. Look at lots of them until you see a format and layout you really like. Then, try to emulate the résumé format using your own information.

Don't get caught up in whether or not you're following a particular résumé formula word-for-word. Use your instincts. If it looks professional, is error-free, and includes all necessary information, then it should be acceptable to the district's Human Resources office.

Just as I said for the cover letter, you should have a few people read through your résumé before you submit it. Ask them to point out mistakes they see and questions they have. Choose someone who will actually look for mistakes, not someone who will read it and say, "It's good."

Scanning Software

Some districts may use "scanning software." This means they might scan your résumé into a computer to search for keywords, or buzzwords. You'll want to be sure your résumé contains the specific words they're looking for.

For example, a school may be in need of a music teacher with experience directing a chorus. After they've scanned all résumés into their computer, they can search for résumé that specifically mention the word "chorus." Music teachers whose résumés include the word "chorus" will appear as preferred candidates.

When you write your résumé, be sure you include very specific keywords and jargon that administrators might search for.

Chapter 9 of this book contains a list of buzzwords that are commonly used by professional educators. You may want to consider incorporating a few of these words into your résumé, if they apply to your situation.

Typing Your Résumé with Microsoft Word

For most people, Microsoft Word can be a real pain when you're typing a résumé. The spacing will be difficult to line up. It'll be hard to set the margins properly. The tab key will take you to random spots on the screen. Fonts will change in the middle of your writing. It will try to automatically number lines that you don't want numbered. And grammar check will put silly green lines under large sections of words that you know are correct.

Be patient and take the time to learn how to design your résumé the right way. If Word is giving you trouble, jump on the Internet and figure out how to fix the problem.

A few word processing tips to help you when designing your résumé:

- Don't use too many fonts in your résumé. Doing so can cause your résumé to seem chaotic and disjointed.

- Keep the spacing even. Use the tab key, not the space bar. This will help you line up columns evenly.

- If you're using Microsoft Word, you might look at the templates to find a résumé that is already designed and formatted. All you'll have to do is plug in your own information.

- You might use bold font to make important places (colleges and schools) stand out. You might use italics to make descriptions of your work stand out.

Common Headings for Teachers' Résumés

- **Objective (Strongly Recommended)**

    Tell what specific subjects and grade levels you're interested in teaching. You can personalize your objective by listing the name of the specific school or district.

- **Certification (Strongly Recommended)**

    Tell what grades and subjects you're certified to teach. List the certificate number so they can look you up. Many employers won't hire candidates who are not fully certified. By listing your certification information, you're reassuring them that there won't be any surprises at the end of the hiring process.

- **Education (Required)**

    What college or university did you attend? You don't need to list your high school. Tell what degree you earned and what you specialized in. If you had a high GPA, list it. If your GPA was not-so-great, don't.

- **Teaching Experience (Required)**

    Include your past teaching jobs and student teaching. (Yes, student teaching does count as <u>real</u> teaching experience.) List names of schools or districts and give a brief summary of your accomplishments.

- **Related Work (Recommended)**

    Any other job(s) you've had that are related to kids or teaching can be included in this section. Include tutoring experience, daycare jobs, or other work that has helped to shape your background. You do not need to include every part-time job you've ever had since you were a teenager —just the ones that are education or child-related.

- **Philosophy (Optional)**

    Adding a teaching philosophy statement can really make you stand out over other candidates. Many people put it near the top of the résumé, or at the very end.

- **Additional Training (Optional)**

    What teacher training have you received besides attending college?

- **Volunteer Work (Optional)**

    Volunteer work always looks good on a résumé, especially when it's related to teaching.

- **Special Skills (Optional)**

    Describe what you're really good at that might be an asset to the district.

- **Publications (Optional)**

    If you've ever written a work that has been published (especially if it's education-related), include it on your résumé. It's an impressive addition to your skill set that most other candidates won't have. Cite your work properly according to MLA or APA standards and offer a brief description.

- **Awards and Honors (Optional)**

    Have you ever received any special honors or awards for outstanding accomplishments? If so, list them in this section. (If you have an honor or award that is college-related, you may want to list it in the "Education" section of your résumé.)

- **References**

    Some people list them, but it's not usually necessary since the reference information will be on the application anyway. You might just say "Furnished upon request."

Sample Résumé

Mary Smith
1234 Beach Road
Youngstown, NY 55512

smith96@aol.com
766-555-7381

My Promise to Students:
I will provide inspirational instruction and compassionate
guidance to foster your academic success and social growth.

Objective

Seeking a position as an elementary classroom teacher (K-4) within the Lewiston School District

Certification

State of New York Permanent Teaching Certification
Elementary Education K-4; Extension Art K-12
Certificate # 1555-12343-A

Education

Daemen College, Buffalo, NY
BA in Elementary Education, December 2008
Minor: Art Studio   GPA: 3.9

Niagara Community College, Niagara Falls, NY
AAS in General Studies, May 2007

Teaching Experience

Youngstown Central Schools, Youngstown, NY   **1/09 – present**
Substitute Teacher
Teach many subjects and grade levels, from Elementary to Middle School. Frequently receive positive feedback from classroom teachers and often requested for future dates.

Martin Luther King School, Kenmore, NY   **11/08 – 12/08**
Student Teacher, 4th Grade
Developed unit plans for math, science, and social studies; taught a novel study; led guided reading groups and literature circles; prepared students for New York State ELA and Math tests.

Teaching Experience

Lincoln Park School, Wheatfield, NY   **9/08 – 11/08**
Student Teacher, 1st Grade
Worked in a self-contained special education classroom; developed unit plans for all subjects; helped coordinate grandparents' breakfast; participated in IEP meetings, parent/teacher conferences, and grade level meetings.

Related Work Experience

Home Music Studio, Youngstown, NY   **1/02 - present**
Music Instructor
Teach private piano, keyboard, and guitar lessons to students in third through ninth grades.

Volunteer Work

Homework Helpers Club, Amherst Boys' and Girls' Club **1/08 - present**
Teacher
Volunteer every Tuesday evening to help students in 6-8th grades with homework. Students receive individualized attention and small group tutoring to assist them with class projects, studying for tests, and daily homework assignments.

Summer Craft Camp, Cheektowaga Parks Service   **1/07 - 1/09**
Camp Counselor
Volunteer for a three-week craft camp for children entering grades 2-5. I designed a daily nature craft activity for students and taught them how to make it.

References

Gladly furnished upon request.

Your Cover Letter and Résumé:
A Matching Pair

Your résumé should match your cover letter. Use the same thick paper. If you had a special letterhead on your cover letter, use it on the résumé as well.

If you have color in your letterhead, it may stand out more. I once had an interviewer say, "You're the person with the blue on your résumé letterhead. Yours caught my eye because nobody ever puts color on their résumés." Obviously you don't want to make your résumé into a tacky rainbow of bold colors, but a subtle dash of green or blue near the top of the page can make you stand out.

If you're not sure how to write a good cover letter and résumé, ask someone to help you. I know I keep repeating this, but it's important: Your documents need to be flawless. No typographical or grammar errors can be allowed. The presentation and spacing needs to be perfect.

If you don't feel confident in your ability to create a good résumé on your own, you may want to hire a service that can create a résumé package for you. A résumé writer will, for a couple hundred dollars or so, ask you a series of questions about your qualifications and then write you a carefully-crafted résumé and cover letter that you can submit to school districts. Some will even give you the digital files so you can edit them as needed in the future. Costs for a résumé and cover letter service can range from $120 up to $500 or more.

No Calls for Interviews? Could Your Cover Letter and Résumé be to Blame?

Many people fail to get called for interviews because their résumé and cover letter aren't written professionally enough. If you've submitted résumés to dozens of schools that are hiring and you don't receive any phone calls, take a second look at your cover letter and résumé.

Usually, when the cover letter and résumé are inadequate, the candidate never really finds out about it. If there are mistakes in your cover letter or résumé, nobody is going to tell you.

Principals won't call to inform you that there are spelling mistakes in your résumé, or the layout of your résumé is awkward, or they didn't understand what you were talking about in your cover letter. Sometimes it's not even about mistakes; sometimes a cover letter is just so boring and plain that it's shuffled off to the side and nobody pays attention to it.

So what do you do? Submit a cover letter with character:

- Be sure it stands out. You don't want a bland letter that blends in among the hundreds of other letters they will receive.

- Be sure you sound excited about becoming a teacher in the body of your letter. Add a sincere sense of enthusiasm.

- Be sure there are no spelling or grammar mistakes in your letter. Embarrassing mistakes can lead administrators to doubt your ability to teach effectively.

- Be sure your résumé 's layout is professional. The formatting and layout should be flawless. It should show that you have an in-depth understanding of how to use Microsoft Word.

- Be sure the information on your résumé is complete. Don't accidentally skip important experiences you have had. Be sure you never, *ever* lie on your résumé.

- Be sure your papers are easy-to-understand, have an attractive layout, and they are so amazing that they cannot possibly be ignored!

- Chapter 5 -

References and Letters of Recommendation

References

Your references will probably be listed on the application you filled out for the school district. If they're not, you may want to include a separate "References" page with your cover letter and résumé. This page should state the names of your references, how you know them, their addresses, phone numbers, and e-mail addresses.

Try to include four or five references. You should use people who have seen your work and will say positive things about you as a teacher.

It is polite to ask people if you can use them as a reference before putting their names down. This gives them a heads-up so they won't be caught off guard if a phone call comes from a school district asking about you.

Letters of Recommendation

You should have three or four letters of recommendation. All letters should be from people you have worked with and who have witnessed your teaching abilities.

Hopefully your cooperating teachers wrote you nice letters when you finished your student teaching. If you've worked in a school before, a letter of recommendation from a principal is ideal. If not, there are still a variety of people you can turn to.

Who should I ask to write my letters of recommendation?

- Principals or Vice-Principals you have worked for (Best!)
- Student teaching cooperating teachers (Excellent!)
- Parents of students you have taught (Very good!)
- Student teaching college supervisors (Good!)
- Other teachers you have worked with (Good!)
- College professors (Good, if you're right out of college!)
- Boss from a non-teaching job (Okay.)
- Friend or neighbor who has not seen you teach (Not that good.)

Some college career centers and school districts try to convince you that you should have people fill out "anonymous letters of recommendation" or "confidential references." Basically, this means you give someone a form to fill out, and they send it back to your potential employer without you seeing it. In other words, it's a letter of recommendation that you never get to read! If possible, don't participate in this. If someone has something good to say about you, you should be able to read it. If they want to say something negative, you should be entitled to know that as well. Unless the district you're applying to requires this (I've heard of very few school districts that do), then just don't do it. If you ask someone to fill out a letter without you seeing it, it's like an open invitation for them to say something you don't want them to.

When you ask someone to write a letter of recommendation for you, give them a copy of your résumé. This will help them include specific and accurate details in their letter.

Give people enough time to write letters of recommendation. You can't ask a person to write a letter and expect a two day turnaround.

If someone agrees to write you a letter and they don't do it within a week or two, it's okay to remind them (in a nice way). Some people need a nudge to get things done.

Be sure to thank people who write letters for you. Writing a good letter is hard work for most people. You might even give them a small token of your appreciation—a small box of chocolates, some homemade cookies, or a thank you card.

Sample Letter of Recommendation

Johnstown Central School District

Lincoln Park School
222 Main Street
Wheatfield, NY 15555
(123) 555-5555

November 28, 2010

It has been my pleasure to work with Mary Smith over the past six weeks. She has been student teaching in my inclusion classroom. There are a number of special needs and ESL students in the class who often require special attention. Given the diversity of this classroom, Mary has acclimated herself remarkably well in a very short period of time.

Mary is a conscientious teacher and works diligently on all aspects of her teaching. She is a cooperative and friendly person who presents herself in a professional manner at all times. She easily built a positive rapport with the students, their parents, and colleagues.

Mary is an effective teacher who has the ability to monitor and adjust her lessons. She asks for feedback, is able to accept constructive criticism, and quickly develops a plan for improvement.

I sincerely believe that Mary will make an outstanding teacher. Her efforts and knowledge are only a few of her good qualities. I'm certain that any district would be lucky to have Miss Smith on their team.

Sincerely,

Mrs. Carol Gray

- Chapter 6 -

Teaching Portfolio:
Your Professional Brag Book

What Is My Teaching Portfolio?

Your portfolio is, quite simply, a large fancy binder that holds all of your important papers and evidence of your best work. It represents who you are as a teacher. Don't get cheap and buy one of those three dollar economy binders at Wal-Mart. You're a professional, so splurge and pay 20 bucks for the nice kind with the leather cover.

What Do I Do With It?

In part, the portfolio is your record keeping binder where you store all of your important teaching papers so you don't lose them. Also, you will use it as a presentation tool when you interview for jobs. You will take your portfolio with you to show evidence of what you have done in the classroom.

(And not only that, you'll look more important when you carry a fancy book of papers into the interview room.)

Do I *Really* Need a Portfolio? I've Heard of People Who Got Jobs Without Having One.

Yes, it's true that people are offered jobs without portfolios. And yes, there's a lot of work involved in assembling a good portfolio. Most of the time interviewers don't even ask to see a portfolio. So, why should you bother?

Here's why: The portfolio can add an interactive dynamic to the interview. A good portfolio is chock full of student work samples, lesson plans, photographs, and philosophy statements. When an interviewer asks you about a given topic, you'll be able to **SHOW** them what you've done.

Think about it: If you're an interviewer, and you're listening to dozens of strangers talk about their successes in education, you're in for a long, dull day. But, if a candidate comes in and **SHOWS** you what they have done, you'll be more engaged. Candidates with a good portfolio have lots of student work to pass around the table. They have photographs of their past experiences. They have copies of their philosophy statement to pass out.

So, do you need a portfolio to land a job? Probably not. Will having a well-stocked portfolio give you a noticeable edge over the competition? Definitely. You'll be the super-prepared candidate who was interesting to listen to and had proof of their teaching experiences.

How Do I Build a Portfolio?

You'll need to buy a fancy binder with a leather cover, lots of sheet protectors (those plastic pocket things that hold papers), and nice-quality divider tabs so you can break your portfolio into sections.

How you design your portfolio is entirely up to you. One way is to make three sections: a table of contents, a section with essential paperwork, and a section with evidence of your teaching.

Table of Contents

Yes, you really do have to make one of these, so don't be lazy. When you're at an interview, you'll want to be sure you can find any paper in ten seconds or less. Your table of contents will not only look professional, but it will be helpful to YOU.

If you want to show an important paper to your interviewer, you don't want thumb through a hundred pages of paperwork saying, "It's in here somewhere."

Section 1: Essential Paperwork

The "essential paperwork" is not the most important part of your portfolio during the interview process, since interviewers should have this information on hand anyway. Still, it's good to have everything ready in case they're missing particular papers, or to refer to if necessary, or in case your interviewers' paperwork is out-of-date. Even though you may not refer to the papers in this section of your portfolio during the interview, it's always better to be prepared.

Also, remember that your portfolio isn't just for job interviews. It's also an organized way of keeping your most important papers related to teaching.

- **Your Résumé**

  This is a summary of who you are. Have an updated copy ready to give to interviewers, in case their copy is out-of-date.

- **List of References**

  Type them out on the same paper and letterhead you used for your résumé and cover letter. Again, this is not hugely important, but it's always good to have an updated reference list on hand.

- **Copy of Your Teaching Certificate**

  Splurge. Spend 99 cents and have it copied in color. It will look so much nicer.

- **Copy of Your College Transcript**

  It's always good to have a copy on hand to show off your high grades in college.

- **Copy of Your College Diploma**

  Again, splurge and have it copied in color for a more professional appearance.

- **Letters of Recommendation**

  Some people have more letters than the Human Resources office requests. Keep them all handy in your portfolio so you can refer to them as needed.

- **Any Other Relevant Awards or Certificates**

  Keep any official papers that you're proud of in your portfolio to show off at your interview.

- **Copies of Your Student Teaching Evaluations**

  Include these only if they're good. You only want to show off your successes.

- **A Short Essay Titled "My Philosophy of Education"**

  Print it out on fancy paper so you can show it to your interviewers when they ask you about it.

Section 2: Evidence of Good Teaching

Now we're getting into the "meat" of your portfolio. These are the items you'll (hopefully) be flipping to and yanking out of your portfolio during the interview. This is your *stuff-*

I-want-to-show-off section. This is filled with actual, physical evidence that you are a good teacher.

- **Three or Four Good Lesson Plans**

  Be sure they're typed and have state or other local education standards listed on them. When they ask you about state standards, pull out your lesson plans and show them.

- **Lesson Plan Observations & Evaluation Forms**

  Again, include these only if you've received high scores. Show off your best work!

- **Samples of Student Work**

  Choose creative and unique projects that you're proud to show interviewers. You're not going to impress them with a boring worksheet. But you may impress them with a Xeroxed copy of a writing project, a science lab journal with a student's observations on it, or a research report. Try to avoid overly simple worksheets or boring, objective tests. You don't want them to think you just do worksheets every day. Show off projects that make students love learning!

- **A Bunch of Photographs**

  You did take some photos during your student teaching, right? Maybe you have a snapshot of a bulletin board you designed or a picture of students working on a project. If you do have pictures, stick them in your portfolio and pass them around the table at your interview. If not, don't worry. It's not a huge deal. But pictures can definitely help bring some positive conversations to the interview table.

- **Copies of a Parent Newsletter**

  You KNOW they'll ask how you communicate with parents. Be prepared to show them! If you don't have any newsletters you've used in the past, make up a sample of what your newsletter *would* look like.

- **Any Other Evidence of Lessons Taught**

  Try to place emphasis on lessons that involve cooperative learning, creative thinking, problem-solving, hands-on manipulation, and/or higher-level thinking skills.

How Do I Use the Portfolio at My Interview?

Some interviewers will ask to see your portfolio and they'll read through it carefully. Others will see that you're carrying it, but never mention it. Even if nobody asks you to see it, you should use your portfolio as a tool for presenting yourself. When you're asked how you have done something, don't just answer the question verbally—show them, using the resources in your portfolio!

Example 1: An interviewer asks you what your classroom rules are. You say, "Let me show you! I have a photograph of a bulletin board I made with classroom rules on it!"

Example 2:   An interviewer asks how you incorporate cooperative learning into your lessons.

You say, "Look at this! I've got a copy of a geometry lesson plan that requires students to work together to find the perimeter of the classroom. I've even got a copy of the lesson evaluation from my cooperating teacher!"

Example 3:   An interviewer asks how you communicate with parents. You say, "I write a weekly parent newsletter to keep parents up-to-date. Let me show you a copy!"

Example 4:   An interviewer asks how you'll handle tough students that refuse to follow school rules. After your answer, you say, "I have a copy of a behavior chart that worked well for one particularly challenging student."

The items in your portfolio give you more control over the interview. The evidence you pull out for "show-and-tell" can be passed around the table, which makes the meeting more interactive for everyone. Also, it allows you to prove that you actually do the things you're talking about.

Top Three Portfolio-Related Mistakes Candidates Make

Mistake #1: They don't have a portfolio. They think they don't need one because their close friend got a job without one. The truth is: yes, many people do get jobs without portfolios. Some principals expect to see a portfolio and some don't. Either way, a candidate with a portfolio will appear more prepared and organized. Candidates with portfolios have a tool they can use to illustrate and prove their experiences. While a portfolio does take time to prepare, if you use it properly, it will definitely give you an edge over the other candidates.

Mistake #2: They don't use their portfolio. Most interviewers will already have a set of questions to ask you. Usually, they don't list, "Show me your portfolio" as one of the questions. You need to be ready to pull out appropriate materials whenever an opportunity arises. If they ask about classroom management—pull out your classroom management plan. If they ask about your teaching philosophy—pull out your philosophy statement. If they ask about differentiated instruction—pull out one of your differentiated lesson plans. If they ask about hands-on projects—pull out photographs of students working on hands-on projects.

Mistake #3: Their portfolio doesn't have enough evidence of their teaching experiences in it. Your résumé, college transcript, and letters of recommendation are NOT the most important parts of a portfolio. Your portfolio should be stuffed with your best lesson plans, lots of student work, and a copious supply of photographs. Chances are you're not going to need to pull out your résumé at an interview—the people interviewing you have already seen it. You're not going to be asked about your college grades or your test scores or your letters of recommendation. You WILL pull out pictures of your teaching, lesson plans, and examples of work that students have done for you.

- Chapter 7 -

Preparing For Your Interview: Common Sense and Professional Advice

Overview of a Typical Interviewing Process

The interviewing process varies from place to place and school to school. Below is a typical interview process for teachers.

At most school districts, teachers generally have to pass several rounds of interviews before they are hired.

Stage 1: Expect a "screening interview," in which you will probably meet with an administrator (usually a school's principal). Sometimes a Human Resources director will conduct the screening interviews.

Stage 2: If you pass the screening interview, you'll be called back for a second interview. This time you'll meet with a large committee, which will include a school principal, a few teachers, and other members of the school staff. They will each take turns asking you specific questions.

Stage 3: If you've made it past the committee, you'll be called back again. This time, they'll probably ask you to teach a sample lesson with a real class of students. (If you interview in the summer when school is out of session, you may get lucky enough to skip this step.)

Stage 4: If you are called back again, the next step is to meet with a higher-level administrator, such as a superintendent or assistant superintendent. If you reach this point in the interview process, this usually means the committee has recommended you as one of the top candidates, and they want to present you as one of their preferred choices for the job.

When You Get the Phone Call

When a school district calls to offer you an interview, remember to politely ASK who will be on the interview panel. If you know the names and positions of those on the panel, you will be able to think about how to phrase your answers to satisfy the interviewers.

For example, if you know there will be a Reading Specialist on the interview committee, then you may want to pay particular attention to strategies for teaching reading. If you find out a Social Worker will be on the panel, you will want to think about ways of dealing with students that have challenging social issues at home and school. And if there happens to be a Special Education teacher on the panel, you can bet on some specific questions that relate to students with special needs.

The most prepared candidates have a good idea of what types of questions will be asked before the interview. If you know who is on the panel, you can have a clear picture of what types of questions will be presented. If you don't ASK, you won't know.

When you ask, write down the names and positions of the members on the panel, if possible. Memorize the administrator's (or other head interviewer's) name. This way, you'll be able to shake their hand and greet them by name when you enter the interview room.

How do you ask about the interview panel politely? Simply say something like, "Thank you for the invitation! I'm very excited to meet with people at your school. Do you mind if I ask who will be conducting the interview?"

The Dos and Don'ts of
Interviewing for a Teaching Job

Interviewing Dos

Dress professionally. Men should wear a nice suit with a jacket. Be sure your tie matches your shirt nicely. Women should wear a conservative dress or business suit.

Practice commonly asked questions before you go to the interview. (Review the practice interview questions in Chapter 8.) If you prepare beforehand, the interview questions will seem routine and familiar. You'll have answers on the tip of your tongue ready-to-go.

> If you prepare beforehand, the interview questions will seem routine and familiar... and you won't be caught off-guard.

The first question at most interviews will be, "Tell us about yourself." You should already know what you're going to say. Keep your answer reasonably brief. The last question will almost always be, "Do you have any questions for us?" Have a thoughtful question ready to ask.

This should go without saying: Be on time. Better yet, be a little early. Fifteen minutes early is ideal.

When you're waiting for your turn in the interview room, smile politely at the people walking by. Be polite to the secretaries in the office. Treat everyone you encounter with respect. You never know who might say something that could influence an interviewer's decisions.

At the interview, be confident, but not cocky. Smile when you walk in. Greet the people interviewing you with a smile and a nod. Firmly shake the hand of the principal and other interviewers that are within easy reach. When you take your seat, sit up straight with your feet on the floor and your hands in a relaxed position on top of the desk.

Address the interviewer by his or her title (Mrs., Miss, Ms., Mr., Dr.) unless you're invited to do otherwise.

Have your teaching portfolio ready. Place your portfolio on the table in front of you when you sit down at the interview table. Usually, the people interviewing you will *not* ask to see your portfolio. Many do, however, expect you to have it on hand. **Don't wait for anyone to mention the portfolio.** Instead, you should use it as a presentation tool to describe your teaching experiences. For example, if you are asked to describe a lesson that involves teaching writing, you might say, "Yes! I can show you... I have a sample of student work that shows how I teach the writing process." (See Chapter 6 for more detailed information about your portfolio.)

Make eye contact. If there are many interviewers at the table, be sure you look at all of them, not just the principal or lead facilitator. You don't want to appear like you're ignoring the rest of the group.

Have a sense of humor. Prepare to make some humorous small talk when you are greeted. For example, if a principal shakes your hand and asks how you are, it's okay to say, "A nervous wreck!" A whimsical introduction can break the ice. Be sure your sense of humor is clean and appropriate for an interview.

Be sure you turn off your cell phone before you enter the school. A ringing cell phone can be embarrassing.

Use lots of examples when you answer questions. When they ask how you **would** do something, tell them how you **already have done** it. This will make you seem more experienced. For example, if an interviewer asks, "How would you use creative problem-solving in your lessons?" Answer with, "When I was student teaching, I did a great creative problem-solving lesson when..." When you use specific examples, you're convincing the interviewers that you're more than just hypothetical talk.

When you leave the interview, remember to thank everyone for meeting with you. Follow up with a letter, addressed specifically to the principal (or other head interviewer), thanking him or her for the opportunity. Send the letter within the next day or two while you are still fresh in his/her mind. (See the sample "Thank You Letter" at the end of this chapter.)

Interview Don'ts

An interview is not the time to use your appearance to express independence or make a unique statement about yourself. Whether you like it or not, you will be judged by your appearance. If you have a nose ring, take it out. If you have a tattoo, cover it up. If you have a bizarre and freaky hair style, change it. You're trying to show interviewers that you're the perfect, well-mannered, clean-cut person who is a good influence on children.

Don't emphasize your weaknesses. Try not to say, "I don't know." Avoid saying, "I'm not really good at..." Don't say, "That's one of my weak points." Always tell the truth, but you don't want to suggest that you're not a confident, successful, qualified teacher. If you are truly unsure how to answer a question, you can ask the interviewer to rephrase the question in a different way.

The job hunting process can be stressful and frustrating, especially if you've been at it for awhile.

Avoid talking about your endless search for jobs. If you've been to dozens of interviews and not gotten a job, don't let them know. If you show your frustrations with the job hunting process, you will seem too desperate, and they may wonder why other schools have turned you down.

Don't tell them you're interested in a school simply because "it is close to home" or it will "reduce your commute time." Singing the praises of the school might get you the job; talking about your commute to work won't.

Don't complain about people. This is not a time to talk about how difficult parents can be, how much your cooperating teacher didn't help you when you student taught, or how your former boss wasn't supportive of his/her staff. If you can't think of nice things to say about people, avoid talking about them at all. Positive, optimistic people will be hired over disgruntled complainers.

Don't slouch. Sit up straight, but don't be too stiff and rigid. Make yourself seem comfortable, but not too casual. Before the interview, practice your posture at your kitchen table if you need to. Your body language says a lot about you.

If you're not offered a job, don't assume they didn't like you. Oftentimes interviewers meet several candidates they like, but can only recommend one person for the job. If they liked you, they may be eager to call you back when the next job opening comes around. Even the very best candidates don't land a job each time they interview.

Don't panic when you read this list of Dos and Don'ts. It may seem overwhelming, but most of the items on this list are really just common sense. Just go in, be comfortable, be relaxed, be polite, be cordial, be prepared, smile, and answer the questions as best you can.

Seven Worst Things To Say at an Interview

1. *"How much will I get paid?"*

    This is a common question to ask at a business interview. Unfortunately, you're not at a business interview. You're interviewing for a teaching job. At most school districts, your salary will be pre-determined by the number of years you've taught and the amount of education you have. Your salary will be discussed when you are formally offered the job. Usually, there is little room for negotiation when you are offered a salary, especially if this is your first teaching job.

2. *"Difficult parents are a challenge."*

    This will lead interviewers to believe you cannot handle difficult parents. You want to seem like you can get along with anybody! They already know parents can be difficult—don't lead the interviewers to believe you're unable to deal with them.

3. *"I'm going to get pregnant in a few months."*

Legally, an interviewer cannot ask you about this. BUT, if you volunteer this information, then they're not going to want to hire you because they'll realize you're going to be taking lots of time off. This is not the time to tell them about your plans to start a family.

4. *"My student teaching experiences weren't that great."*

If they ask you about your student teaching experiences, tell them how wonderful your cooperating teachers were, how great it was to teach the kids, and how much you've grown professionally. This is not the time to complain or make excuses for any of your teaching experiences. Try not to complain about anyone (cooperating teachers, students, parents, former colleagues, etc.) during an interview. If your student teaching experience didn't go well, you can be honest, but don't blame the cooperating teacher, and try to put a positive spin on the situation by telling how much you learned.

5. *"I have a hard time making kids behave."*

Principals are looking for teachers who are low-maintenance. They want teachers that know how to manage a classroom effectively, with minimal disruptions in learning. They don't want to deal with kids in the office for misbehaving. They certainly don't want to deal with angry parents calling the school. Yes, your primary job is to teach, but an administrator will be very afraid to hire anyone that cannot manage discipline problems effectively, fairly, and independently.

6. *"I'm applying for this job because I am new in town. My spouse moves around a lot."*

This sends a red flag to interviewers because they are looking for people who will stay around awhile. Also, it is letting the interviewer know that you consider your job as secondary to your spouse's. Because teaching is a professional, career-level job, long-term commitment is important. If you have moved around a lot, you can tell the interviewer the truth. But be sure to add, "We love it here and we plan to settle in this area permanently now." Let them know you want to retire as a teacher in their district!

7. *"I'm not too good with computers."*

In this day and age, schools are largely centered on technology. You'll be expected to use e-mail every day to correspond with colleagues, fill out report cards via electronic grading systems, use databases to look up student information, and take attendance on computers. You'll also be expected to use up-to-date technology in your lessons and even teach computer literacy! Computers are such an integral part of education today, you will not get hired without some level of computer knowledge.

Seven Tips for Teaching a Demonstration Lesson

If you do well, and the interview committee is seriously considering you as one of the final candidates, you may be invited back to teach a demonstration lesson (or a sample lesson). This is usually a 10 – 20 minute lesson in front of real students. Below are six thoughts to consider when planning your demonstration lesson:

- From the demonstration lessons I've observed, the number one problem people have is keeping it within the given time frame. Since sample lessons are usually very short, there's no way you're going to fit much in. Do what you can in a very short time frame.

- Whatever you teach, be sure it is review or builds on something kids already know. Interviewers are basically looking to see how well you interact with students and how kids respond to your lessons. They're not looking for students to learn amazing new things. If you try to teach them a new concept, they might be confused — and this wouldn't make you seem like the top-quality teacher you really are.

- If possible, make your sample lesson a hands-on activity. Students often learn best by "doing." Try to incorporate some kind of manipulative materials. Interviewers know that these lessons involve preparation and planning. Your extra effort will be noticed.

- Have any necessary supplies and materials prepackaged in Zip-Lock bags or another type of small container. You don't want to waste valuable minutes passing out supplies and cleaning up.

- Be sure your directions to students are clear, simple, and presented in an organized way. Your lesson should have a brief introduction, a hands-on or interactive activity, and a brief closure discussion. You won't have time to accomplish a lot, but an organized lesson structure can make even the shortest lesson seem complete.

- Write up a lesson plan and give a copy to each interviewer that is observing your lesson. Your lesson plan should be typewritten. State standards should be listed on the lesson plan.

- Relax and have fun. Try to let your personality shine through. Don't be afraid to show a sense of humor when communicating with students. If you're relaxed and confident, the interviewers will notice!

Sample Thank You Letter

Mary Smith
1234 Beech Road
Youngstown, NY 55512

smith96@aol.com
708-352-7381

Mr. Michael Green
Lewiston Elementary School
123 Main Street
Lewiston, NY 55513

June 15, 2010

Dear Mr. Green,

Thank you for taking the time to meet with me for an interview yesterday. Please extend my thanks to the other teachers and staff who were on the interview committee.

I was extremely impressed with Lewiston Elementary's positive education environment and its focus on student success. It was clear that the school is a place where students feel safe and comfortable. The warm, friendly attitudes of you and your staff made me feel at ease. Your students are lucky to attend such a wonderful school.

Again, thank you for the interview. I look forward to hearing from you soon.

Sincerely,

Mary Smith

- Chapter 8 -

Fifty Common Interview Questions (and How to Answer Them)

Interview questions for teaching jobs usually are not unique or creative. Some variation of the same set of general questions is asked by almost every interview committee. Even though the words in the questions may be changed slightly, a prepared candidate will be familiar with the types of questions that will come up.

Use the 50 sample questions below to prepare for your interview. Depending on your learning style, you may want to write out answers for yourself to study, or you might want to practice with a friend or family member. Just be sure you know how to answer each question below with confidence.

1. Tell us about yourself.

This will be the first question at almost every interview. Just give a brief background in about three sentences. Tell them what colleges you graduated from, what you're certified to teach, what your teaching and working experiences are, and why you'd love the job.

2. How do you teach to the state standards?

If you interview in the United States, you'll find that school administrators love to talk about state, local, or national standards! Reassure them that everything you do ties into standards. Be sure the lesson plans in your portfolio have the state standards typed right on them. When they ask about them, pull out a lesson plan and show them the close ties between your teaching and the standards.

3. How will you prepare students for standardized assessments?

There are standardized assessments at almost every grade level. Be sure you know the names of the specific tests your students will be required to take. Talk about your experiences preparing students. You'll get bonus points if you know and describe the format of the test because that will prove your familiarity with the assessments.

4. Describe your discipline philosophy.

Most effective teachers use lots of positive reinforcement. They are firm, but you don't yell. Hopefully you have appropriate consequences for inappropriate behavior. You may want to mention that you have your classroom rules posted clearly on the walls. You set common routines that students follow every day. And, of course, you adhere to the school's discipline guidelines.

Also, it's important to emphasize that you suspect discipline problems will be minimal because your lessons are very interesting and engaging to students. Kids tend to misbehave when they're bored and when they're not sure what they're supposed to be doing. A good teacher will always have the students engaged in interesting lessons and he/she will communicate expectations clearly.

Never tell the interviewer that you "send kids to the principal's office" whenever there is a problem. You should be able to handle most discipline problems on your own.

5. What do you do when a student is a <u>serious</u> discipline problem?

The answer is similar to #4, but you should emphasize that you follow through with the school's discipline procedures. You need to make the principal aware of all serious issues. If the child is a physical threat to other students, you have him or her removed immediately. You involve social workers or counselors when necessary.

When you have a "tough student" in your class, you need to be prepared to deal with him or her on a daily basis. You can use a behavior modification plan for on-going behavior problems. This would require you to keep a record of student behaviors throughout the day (perhaps in the form of a checklist). You can then offer the student a reward for a good behavior report and/or a consequence for a bad report.

Behavior modification plans allow you as a teacher to monitor the progress of the student. They can serve as a communication link between school and home for parents. And they allow students to see and reflect on their own progress.

6. What is your favorite subject to teach?

Elementary teachers get asked this a lot. If you're in an elementary school where you will be teaching all subjects, then tell them your favorite is reading, writing, or math. Most administrators think these are the most important subjects because they are the basis to all learning. It's okay to like science and social studies too, but be sure they know you have a passion for teaching math, reading, and writing. If you're in a middle school or high school, you may be asked to describe your favorite unit or topic within your subject area.

7. How do you motivate students to learn?

Your lessons are all exciting. If you're in elementary school, your lessons are fun, hands-on, and manipulative. Show them an example of an interactive lesson in your portfolio. If you're in high school, you keep your lessons interesting by presenting students with thought-provoking challenges. You do a lot of cooperative learning activities where kids can work together. You might also emphasize that you connect your lessons to real-life events that students can relate to. As always, back up your words with examples and evidence.

8. How do you meet the needs of special education students?

If they have an IEP (Individualized Education Plan), you follow it. (You'll get bonus points for using the acronym "IEP.") You work together with the special education teacher to find out what the student needs and to provide it to him/her. You modify your assignments so that the special education child is challenged, but not overwhelmed. Give an example (without using names) of a special needs student you've worked with in the past. Tell what you did to help that child reach his or her fullest potential.

9. How do you integrate technology into your teaching?

You take the students to the computer lab. You use word processors with students. You teach students to use the Internet for research projects. You tell them you're anxious to put up a classroom website. If you've ever used CPS Clickers, tell them about it. If you've ever used a PowerPoint in your teaching, tell them about it. You can even take it one step further and tell them you'd think it would be fun to teach the kids to make their *own* PowerPoint presentations. If you have experience using a SmartBoard or electronic whiteboard, be sure to mention this as well.

10. How do you make reading and writing a part of your science (or social studies or whatever) lesson?

Reading and writing is a part of every subject because it is the foundation for learning. All teachers are teaching reading and writing every day. Give examples of how you have taught reading and writing in science class. And in social studies. And math. And home economics. And Spanish. And whatever you're going to be teaching.

11. Why do you want to teach at this particular school?

When you are asked this question, be prepared to flatter their pants off. Tell them: You love this school and this is where your heart is. This is where your dreams are. This school just happens to be in the community you want to live in. You can't say enough good things about the student population. It's wonderful because the parents are so involved here. You've known other teachers in the district who are very happy here. If you've student taught or subbed in this school, tell them how marvelous your experiences were. Let them know that you've applied to a couple of schools, but this school is by far your number one choice.

Don't talk about how your commute will be shorter. Interview committees don't care about your commute. Keep singing the praises of the school when you answer this question, and avoid talking about yourself.

12. What do you do if a student confides in you and tells you about a serious problem (example: they tell you they are being abused), but asks you not to tell anyone?

You report it. For the student's safety, you must tell an appropriate authority. Depending on the school's policy, you might tell a social worker, counselor, or principal. Most students will understand that you're trying to make things better. If they're confiding in you, that means they're looking for a solution. Since you cannot take this kind of matter into your own hands, reporting the incident is your way of helping the student find a solution to the problem.

13. How do you integrate higher-level thinking skills into your teaching?

You present students with open-ended assignments that require creativity and advanced thinking skills. Your test questions often feature subjective questions that require reasoning and logic. You challenge students to "discover" answers, rather than just tell them answers. Present examples from your portfolio.

14. How do you integrate creative problem-solving skills into your teaching?

You welcome creative thinking and don't expect a single right/wrong answer from each student. You pose challenging questions or thoughts and give students the resources to come up with a unique solution.

Creative problem-solving can also be taught as a process. When students are given a problem to solve, they can brainstorm solutions (on their own or with a group). Then, they use logic and critical thinking to narrow down their brainstormed list and choose the best possible solution for their problem. This type of problem-solving lesson really exercises students' creativity.

15. What is your philosophy on teaching math?

You want students to "discover" math. If you're in an elementary school, emphasize manipulatives. Elementary teachers teach math using Unifix Cubes, Place Value Blocks, Counters, Judy Clocks, and Geoboards. (If you don't know what these things are, do a Google search.) Elementary teachers should know the difference between the "Everyday

Math Program" (which is "New Math") and a more traditional math program.

Secondary teachers must emphasize the teaching of concepts in interesting ways that will keep students engaged. Give specific examples of ways you connect math to real-life situations that kids can relate to. Also, emphasize that all instruction is aimed at preparing students for state assessments.

16. What is your philosophy on teaching science?

No matter what grade you teach, science should have a hands-on emphasis. Your teaching should involve lots of exploration, experiments, and demonstrations. Be prepared with examples in your portfolio.

17. What is your philosophy on teaching social studies?

They're looking to see if you make history come alive. Maybe you create fun lessons where kids dress up as historical figures. Maybe you have them make models of historical places and things. Maybe you have the students act out historical scenarios. Maybe you have kids make their own geographical salt maps. Maybe you show them ways that history has made the world the way it is today. Your philosophy should suggest that you do whatever it takes to make social studies interesting to students.

Also, at all grade levels, literature can be used to teach history. For example, if you're interviewing for a middle school social studies job, you can tell them how much you love using *Diary of Anne Frank* to teach students about World War II.

18. How do you use literature in your teaching?

In all grades, your reading instruction should incorporate great literature. If you want to impress the interviewers with this question, throw out the names of very <u>specific books</u> you have used in your teaching. If you're in an elementary school, for example, you might tell them you love to read Judy Blume's *Fudge* books to your class or that you're a huge fan of R.L. Stine's *Goosebumps* and you just can't get enough of Eric Carle's picture books! If you'll be teaching English in a middle school or high school, you could tell the interviewers how you're passionate about teaching kids to read the standard classics like J.R.R. Tolkien's *The Hobbit* and Steinbeck's *Of Mice and Men*. The key to answering this question well is to show an enthusiasm toward teaching literacy, and also back it up with the names of specific literary works you might use in your classroom.

19. Why did you decide to become a teacher?

It's not because you like having the summer off! Perhaps you became a teacher because you love learning or because you've always loved school. Maybe people in your family are teachers, and you've picked up your talent for teaching from them. Perhaps you are extremely passionate about sharing your wisdom with students and watching young minds blossom.

20. Where do you see yourself in five years?

They're checking to see if this is a career commitment for you. You see yourself in the classroom in five years! You can't imagine being anywhere else. Or, perhaps, you plan to pursue an administration degree and advance your career within the district. Whatever you do, don't imply that the job you're applying for is a short-term steppingstone to a job in another district.

Notable Quote

"I had a job interview at an insurance company once and the lady said, 'Where do you see yourself in five years?' and I said, 'Celebrating the fifth anniversary of you asking me this question.'"

- Mitch Hedberg, American Comedian 1968 - 2005

---

21. What are your strengths?

This one's easy enough. It's your chance to toot your own horn. You are such a great teacher because ___. Show pictures, lessons, and evaluations from your portfolio of something you do very well.

22. What are your weaknesses?

This is probably one of the most common interview questions in any professional interview. I want to go into a little more depth with this question because it's so tricky for most people. Some people believe that you should never expose your real weaknesses if you want to pass an interview. I disagree. It's okay to be open and honest about your weaknesses, but just don't get carried away and sound too extreme.

Interviewers are looking for two things: First, they want to see if you are able or willing to grow out of your weaknesses and learn from them. Second, they're looking to be sure your weaknesses aren't so extreme that they'll affect your ability to teach effectively.

I have seen candidates perform extremely well through an entire interview, just to lose the job because of the weaknesses question. This happens when people admit too much about their weaknesses, or they make it sound like they're unable to handle key aspects of the job.

What types of answers should you avoid?

1. Major discipline issues. You won't be hired if the principal thinks you will have trouble keeping kids under control. It's okay to admit that quieting down the class can be a challenge once in awhile, but don't imply that you won't have your class under control.

2. Major problems dealing with people (parents, colleagues, etc.) can also raise red flags. Some people have a knack for getting other people all riled up. If you suggest that you're the kind of teacher that's going to get parents and colleagues angry, you won't get the job. Again, if you say your weakness is occasional stubbornness on certain issues you should be fine. But don't imply that you're the kind of person who can never get along with anyone.

3. This last one applies to elementary school teachers only. Your major weakness should not be an inability to teach math, reading, or writing well. Principals will usually see these subjects as a foundation for all other learning. If you can't teach these well, you will not be perceived as a strong teacher. However, if your

weakness is simply having difficulty assigning objective grades to writing assignments, that's not nearly as severe as saying, "I don't have a clue how to teach reading."

When you talk about your weaknesses, be honest with the interviewers, but also avoid anything that implies you have extreme deficiencies in your ability to teach.

One more important point regarding the weakness question: Whenever you state a weakness, be sure you follow up with a plan for improvement. You want to show that you're constantly growing as a teacher and as a professional. You don't want them to think you have a weakness that you're not going to do anything about.

Consider implementing the following formulas for answering the weakness question:

- One of my weaknesses is _(your weakness)_, but I have learned to _(solution)_.

   or, a more advanced version of the same formula:

- One of my weaknesses was _(weakness)_, but _(person)_ taught me to overcome this by _(solution)_. Now, I _(how you're better)_.

23. How would you handle a gifted student?

They're looking to see what you would do with a gifted student in your own classroom. How would you challenge the student, so he or she does not become bored with school. You want to ensure that they're learning as much as they possibly can.

There are a couple of answers that candidates give all the time that are just plain wrong:

- Not-so-great answer #1: "I will give the student extra work."

    Don't say you'll give them extra work because you don't want to punish the child for being gifted.

    Better answer: "I will modify assignments to make them more challenging. Differentiated instruction is the key to ensuring that all students are challenged."

- Not-so-great answer #2: "I will have the gifted child help other students who are struggling."

    Don't say that you will have the child "help struggling students" because that implies that you'll use the child as your little servant-tutor because they finished their work too fast.

    Better answer: "I will provide individualized attention and/or small-group instruction when possible so that children at all ability levels can maximize their learning. I will make the assignments more challenging and encourage gifted students to use advanced problem-solving skills and higher-level thinking."

24. What is the biggest challenge you've had to overcome in your life?

This probably has very little to do with how good of a teacher you are, but interviewers like to ask oddball stuff like this. Other variations of this question might be, "Who has had the biggest influence on your life?" and "What do you like to do in your free time?" Be ready to answer strange questions like that.

25. What is the last book you read?

They love to ask this one too. Obviously you don't want to say, "I haven't read any books lately." Tell them you're an avid reader. Name a book. Tell them how much you're into it right now.

26. Do you use cooperative learning in your classroom?

Of course you do! Give examples of times when you've had students work together in pairs or groups. Better yet, show them pictures and lesson plans in your portfolio.

You may want to mention that when you have students participate in cooperative learning, you assign them specific jobs or tasks to keep each member of the group involved. Also, you'll want to tell them how you monitor the groups to ensure everyone's on the right track.

27. How do you communicate with parents?

This question will come up at almost every elementary school interview. It's fairly common at the middle school and high school level as well. Perhaps you send home a weekly or monthly parent newsletter. (Pull out an example of a newsletter from your portfolio.) Some teachers even publish assignments, homework help, and newsletters on a classroom website. (If you do this, print out a copy of your website and stick it in your portfolio.)

For grades 3 and up, you may require students to have an assignment book that has to be signed each night. This way, parents know what assignments are given and when projects are due. When there are discipline problems, you might call home and talk to parents. Some teachers invite parents to communicate via email. It's important to have an open-door policy and invite parents to share their concerns at any time.

While it is important to keep parents informed of any problems a child is having in school, positive communication is important too! Sending congratulatory notes home to parents shows that you notice when a student does well!

28. In what ways would you help out with extracurricular activities?

You'll coach sports, help out with PTA fundraisers, become Chess Club adviser, chaperone dances, direct the school play, and sit in the dunk tank on Field Day! Think about what extracurricular activities the school has and tell them which ones you happen to be interested in.

Elementary schools will often prefer candidates who are willing to volunteer for after-school events and activities. Many high schools and middle schools will prefer candidates who are willing to coach or become an adviser for a club.

At all grade levels, a teacher who is willing to stay after school to help students with academic school work is seen as a big plus. Administrators love to see teachers offer after-school help sessions!

29. Would you be open to a team-teaching situation?

Every school seems to have a different definition of team-teaching. At some schools it means sharing a classroom. At others it means block scheduling. In some elementary schools, it means you switch classes for a period or two. In an inclusion classroom, it might mean regular education and special education teachers co-teach. First, figure out what "team-teaching" means to the interviewer; then tell them what an exciting opportunity it would be.

30. Do you feel it is appropriate for kids to be using the Internet in school? If so, how can you protect them from inappropriate websites?

The Internet is a wonderful teaching resource for students, but they must be monitored closely. When possible, teachers should specify which sites students should be on at any given time during class. Never give students free reign of the computers. When you're in the computer lab, you should give students specific tasks or websites to visit. Most schools already have filters installed on their computers, but they cannot be used as a substitute for close adult supervision.

31. In what ways will you communicate with administration?

Principals don't like to be left in the dark. They like to be kept informed of all the wonderful things that are going on in your classroom. Tell them that you will drop a copy of your weekly/monthly parent newsletter in their mailbox. You can also make sure the principal gets a copy of each parent note you send home with your class. Reassure them that you are an easy person to talk to and you will keep him or her up-to-date on all the major events going on in your classroom.

32. How will you use the writing process in your teaching?

The writing process can be used whenever you want to have students create a complete, well-written piece of work. It consists of several steps:

1. Brainstorming ideas (or using a graphic organizer)
2. Writing a draft copy
3. Proofreading (peer editing or teacher correcting)
4. Writing a final copy
5. Presenting the work (hanging it up, sharing with class, etc.)

No matter what subject or grade you're teaching, there should be countless ways to incorporate the writing process.

A few things to consider when they ask you about the writing process:

- Graphic organizers (like webs, sequence chains, Venn diagrams, or t-charts) are all the rage these days. They allow students to organize and prepare their writing. Explain how you will use them when you use the writing process. Better yet, stick an example or two in your portfolio to show off.

- Peer editing checklists work especially well. This allows students to work in cooperative groups to improve and correct their own writing. Again, you might want to stick an example of a peer editing checklist in your portfolio.

- Presenting or publishing the work is extremely important. Without this work, the student is simply creating work for the purpose of "handing it in." By hanging the work on the wall, allowing students to share it with the class, presenting it to parents, or publishing it in a newsletter, you're giving the students an exciting purpose for writing.

33. What can you contribute to our teaching team here at this school?

This is a wide open question. Tell them what you're good at and how it will benefit them. Your response should be somewhat specific so they know you've got a skill to offer that they don't already have on the team. Maybe you're really good at teaching with computers. Maybe you're an expert in Shakespeare. Maybe you did your Master's thesis on classroom discipline techniques. Maybe you're really crafty and can display student work in artsy and clever ways. When you answer this question, you want the interviewers to think, "Oh! We need someone like you around here."

34. What will your classroom environment look like?

Interviewers ask this question often. Some people talk about the student work hanging on the walls and the arrangement of furniture. There's a trick to answering this question: Don't just describe your room, but describe the *students* in the room. Your classroom environment is filled with busy, happy students participating in hands-on, exploratory learning.

35. How much homework do you give?

Students do have other responsibilities after school (tae-kwon do, family dinner, sports, Scouts, music lessons). Kids should have some homework to build responsibility and learning outside the classroom, but you don't want to overwhelm them.

You might want to describe the rule of 10s: Teachers should give no more than *grade level times ten*. In other words, if you teach third grade: 3 x 10 = 30 minutes of homework. Fourth graders should have less than 40 minutes. Fifth graders should have less than 50 minutes. High school teachers might want to be careful if using this formula—120 minutes of homework (12th graders) is too much for any student!

36. Describe a college course you've taken that has made you a stronger teacher.

Choose a course that directly relates to teaching. You can answer with almost anything— a classroom management course, a class about teaching reading, or whatever. Describe how the professor connected theory to reality. Tell how he or she opened your eyes to the realities of teaching in a positive way. Then, show how you've used this information in your student teaching or other experience.

37. How were your student teaching experiences?

You had wonderful student teaching experiences. Reach into your portfolio and pull out a copy of the letter of recommendation that your cooperating teacher wrote for you. Explain how wonderful the students were and how much you enjoyed teaching a unit on ___. Tell them you were fortunate to have been placed in such good schools. If your student teaching school was similar to the school you're interviewing in, compare the two schools' positive attributes. Whatever you do, when you answer this question, keep your answer positive!

38. How do you feel about an inclusion classroom?

Inclusion means special education students will be included in a regular education setting. Teaching in an inclusion classroom may require modifying assignments, working with disabled students and/or students with behavioral challenges. Oftentimes, inclusion teachers are partnered with a special education teacher during instruction times.

The main goal of an inclusion program is to challenge special needs students, just as you would other students, in the regular classroom for some or all of the school day. You need to be willing to ensure that all students have the same social and academic opportunities.

If you are open to working in an inclusion classroom, you'll want to emphasize your experiences working with special needs students. Also, show off your abilities to differentiate instruction and challenge all students according to their abilities. Familiarity with specific disabilities and the workings of special education programs (writing IEPs, attending CSE meetings, etc.) are a big plus.

39. How do you feel about being paired up with a mentor?

Most school districts have a mentoring system in place. You will probably be assigned a mentor who will walk you through your first year of teaching. Tell them you would appreciate their mentor program because you value the insight and constructive criticism that veteran teachers can provide.

40. What is your philosophy of education?

This question is very broad, yet it can reveal a great deal about your personality and how you will act as a teacher. Some interviewers insist that it is the most important question they can ask. Think this question through carefully. Also, have a short (one page) narrative that answers this question available in your portfolio.

41. What would you do if a student is consistently not handing in homework?

Describe your homework policy. If a student refuses to hand in homework assignments on a regular basis, you would probably conference with the student and contact parents. You also need to consider why the child does not hand in assignments on-time. If the student is missing assignments because the work is too difficult, you would offer to help the child after school or during a free period. If the student is unorganized (not writing the assignments down or losing copies of assignments), you might assign the student a "study buddy" within the class and/or suggest organization techniques.

42. What are the biggest challenges for teachers today?

Be careful when answering this question. It's not a green light to complain about the many needs of special education students or the struggles of dealing with difficult parents. The interview committee does not want to hear complaining. They're looking for you to identify a few things that will be hard to do and then say that you will face the challenges head-on. For example: "One of the biggest challenges is making sure I meet the academic and emotional needs of all students in my class, even when they're at different academic levels." (Then, of course, quickly point out that you are prepared to do this.)

43. List three characteristics of an effective teacher.

This is a common question and a relatively easy one to answer. Just pick some creative adjectives and phrases that describe a great teacher. Then, be sure to describe how each one relates to your own teaching experiences. Some good examples include:

1. Caring
2. Good classroom manager
3. Prepared for anything
4. Knowledgeable
5. Able to communicate with others (students, co-workers, parents, and community)
6. Hardworking
7. Flexible
8. Creative
9. Able to connect with kids

44. How do you make sure you meet the needs of a student with an IEP?

An IEP is an "Individualized Education Plan." Students with special needs will be given an IEP, or a list of things that you must do when teaching the child. An IEP might include anything from "additional time for testing" to "needs all test questions read aloud" to "needs to use Braille textbook." How do you ensure you're meeting the needs of a student with an IEP? First, read the IEP carefully. If you have questions, consult a special education teacher, counselor, or other staff member who can help you. Then, you just make sure you follow the requirements on the IEP word for word. When necessary, you may be asked to attend a meeting in which you can make suggestions for updating the IEP. Your goal, and the goal of the IEP, is to make sure the student has whatever he or she needs to be successful in your class.

45. Give an example of a differentiated assignment you might give.

Differentiated instruction is a huge buzzword these days. Basically, it means that you change your instruction based on the needs of individual students or groups of students. The interviewer is looking for an example of a lesson where each student is not doing the exact same assignment, the same way. The students' assignments will all be based on a common theme or concept being taught, but each student's requirements will vary depending on his or her ability and learning style.

46. Do you love working with children?

You're probably thinking, "Well, duh! I'm a teacher. Of course I like working with kids." Truth is, your interviewer knows that many people become burned out with teaching because they discover they don't like working with kids. Reassure your interviewer that you love working with kids and that this is your dream job. Then, go on to tell him or her why you like working with kids. Tell them that you enjoy sharing your knowledge or you find pleasure in the unique challenges that change every day. Tell them you love answering kids' questions and that you have special ways of showing you care.

47. What do you look for in an administrator?

If you know anything about the principal that's interviewing you, try to mention their strengths in your reply. A few things you might like to see in a principal can include presence in the classroom, interaction with students, being supportive of teachers, showing an interest in student learning, being easily accessible, and creating a positive school environment.

48. Have you subbed in our district?

It's not uncommon for an administrator to hire people that already have a foot in the district's door. If you've been a successful sub in the school, the principal can easily check with teachers in the school to see how you did. Furthermore, it shows you're serious about wanting to work for that particular district. If you have not subbed, tell them the truth, but reassure them that your experiences are solid and your commitment is real. (If you don't already have a full-time teaching job, it's always a good idea to get on a school's substitute list whenever possible. This will ensure you're employed until you do get a full-time teaching job, and it will also help you to build up your résumé.)

49. How do you assess students? Describe your tests and quizzes.

You can answer this question by saying that you use a variety of assessment strategies. If applicable, remind the interviewer that your in-class assessments reflect and prepare students for state or standardized testing. Also, let them know that you include test questions that involve higher-order thinking skills (like short answer questions, essay questions, questions that involve graphic organizers, etc.) Many teachers also find informal assessments—such as in-class questioning and student interviews—effective. You might also assess student projects or reports, in addition to traditional tests. Again, this is a good time to reflect on the increasing need to prepare students for state testing. Tell your interviewer how your tests parallel the state's exams and how your tests can help you to accurately pinpoint your students' strengths and weaknesses. Good instruction is guided by the results of student assessments.

50. Do you have any questions for us?

This is the final question of almost every interview. Be prepared with a thoughtful question ahead of time. You might want to butter them up by saying something cheesy like, "What are you most proud of at this school?" (It really IS a great question to ask.) Or, you might try something like, "Many parents and community members speak very highly of this district, which is why I was so eager to come to meet with you today. In your opinion, why is this school so highly regarded?" If you're too embarrassed to throw out cheesy questions loaded with compliments, you could ask, "Can you tell me about the people I will be working most closely with?"

When they ask if you have any questions, don't answer with, "Nope." These people will be meeting with lots of candidates today. This is your chance to say something that will make you stand out. On top of that, asking a question shows you're serious about wanting the job. And no matter how cheesy your comments sound, it'll make them smile because it's complimentary. And think about it: You've been in the hot seat, answering *their* questions, for 45 minutes. You've earned the right to turn the table, even if it is just for a moment.

- Chapter 9 -

Teacher Jargon, Acronyms, and Buzzwords

When you interview, you'll want to be able to use and understand up-to-date teacher jargon. If an interviewer asks about your opinions on looping or how you use differentiated instruction, you don't want to be the candidate who says, "Huh? Can you rephrase the question?"

You need to have an educator's vocabulary. Before your interview, you'll want to brush up on all those buzzwords you learned in college. If you casually speak fluent teacher jargon and use key words at appropriate times in their appropriate contexts, then you are certain to leave a positive impression on the interviewers.

The following list is not meant to be a complete compilation of buzzwords that might be used in an interview, but should be a helpful resource to get you thinking about the kinds of words you should be able to use and talk about.

To prepare yourself for an interview, try this practice activity:

Use each word below in a sentence and relate it to your teaching abilities. Underline any terms you are unfamiliar with and look them up before you attend an interview.

1. Assessment
2. Advanced Placement (High School)
3. Basic Facts (Elementary Mathematics)
4. Behavior Modification Plan (or Behavior Modification Chart)
5. Best Practices
6. Block Scheduling (Middle or High School)
7. Bloom's Taxonomy
8. Conflict Resolution
9. Cooperative Learning
10. Creative Problem-Solving
11. Critical Thinking
12. Curriculum Map
13. DEAR - Drop Everything and Read (Elementary School); aka SSR or Silent Sustained Reading
14. DIBELS Reading Assessment (Early Childhood)
15. Differentiated Instruction
16. Everyday Mathematics (Elementary)
17. ESL Students - English as a Second Language (or ELL, English Language Learners)
18. Four Block Literacy (Elementary)

19. Four Square Writing (Elementary)
20. GATE - Gifted and Talented Education
21. Graphic Organizer
22. Higher-Order Thinking Skills
23. IEP - Individualized Education Plan or Individualized Education Program
24. Inclusion
25. Informal Reading Inventory (Elementary)
26. Inquiry-Based Learning Methods
27. Mastery Learning
28. Mentor Teacher
29. Multicultural Education
30. Leadership
31. Learning Styles
32. Literature Circles (Elementary)
33. Looping
34. Manipulatives (Elementary Mathematics)
35. Mentor Program
36. Multi-Age Grouping
37. Multiple Intelligences
38. National Board Certification
39. Phonics (Elementary)
40. Pull-out versus Push-in Instruction
41. RTI - Response to Intervention
42. Rubric
43. Scientific Method
44. SmartBoard
45. Special Needs
46. Standards or State Standards
47. State Testing or Standardized Testing
48. Team Teaching
49. Whole Language (Elementary)
50. Writing Process

- Chapter 10 -

Will I Ever Get Hired?

If you don't get a job right away, don't give up. I've been on lots of interview committees where we've interviewed several amazing candidates who all deserved to be hired. Unfortunately, when there are not enough positions available, even excellent candidates will not be hired. Even the best teachers usually have to interview at several schools before they land a job.

Just keep applying. Spread your résumé to school districts all around your area. Be patient and try not to let the waiting make you crazy. I know it's tough, especially when you're eager to begin teaching and when you need to earn money to keep your financial head above water.

In the meantime, you'll want to keep building on your experiences. You don't want an obvious gap in your résumé that shows you've finished school and obtained your teaching degree, but have remained unemployed for one year, two years, or more.

If you find yourself without a full-time teaching job, you can still build your experiences by becoming a sub. Substitute teaching jobs are usually a little easier to obtain, provide a fair salary, and offer wonderful opportunities to work directly with students in the school setting.

Benefits of Substitute Teaching

1. You get to network and meet lots of teachers and administrators!

2. You'll get to sample a variety of grade levels and subjects to discover which is best for you.

3. You can sub in more than one school district and discover which ones suit you the best.

4. You'll have a more flexible schedule!

5. Opportunities for long-term substitute positions arise all the time. Taking over for someone on a leave of absence is just like having a full-time teaching job.

In the competitive education job market, you'll need to work very hard to win your job of choice. The process will involve many months of writing business letters, copying paperwork, mailing out application packets, making follow-up phone calls, studying for interviews, perfecting your teaching portfolio, and going on several rounds of interviewing. Searching and applying for jobs can seem like a full-time job in and of itself.

If you become frustrated, think about your goal! This is your first step to a long, rewarding teaching career. You've endured years of college-level training. You've passed your student teaching. Maybe you've even endured subbing. All of your hard work will pay off when you get the key to your new classroom. Then, you'll be on your way to enriching the lives of students with your teaching skills.

If you work hard, teach with passion, and maintain a professional relationship with your students, parents, administrators, and colleagues, a full-time teaching job will eventually find you.

Once you've landed the job of your dreams, you will enjoy your career for many, many years to come. You'll look back at your job hunting experiences and remember the long, involved process you endured, and hopefully, you'll know it was well worth the effort.

- Chapter 11 -

Advice and Inside Information from Three Interview Experts

Now that you've read my thoughts, advice, and strategies for getting the teaching job of your dreams, I would like you to hear about the experiences and opinions of other "interview experts" who are also extremely familiar with the teacher hiring process.

Interview Expert #1:
Wendy's Experience as a Candidate

First, I would like you to meet Wendy from Southeastern Pennsylvania. After interviewing at nine schools, she landed a job as a middle school science teacher. Being from Pennsylvania, Wendy was competing for a sought-after job in a suburban public school. How did she do it? I'll let you read the interview in her own words:

Tim: *Let's start with a little background information. What city do you live in? What's the job market like in your area?*

Wendy: I live near Downingtown/West Chester in Chester County, Pennsylvania, west of Philadelphia. It is very competitive—a growing suburban area with excellent public schools. The districts receive hundreds of applications for each job. Pennsylvania has a strong teachers' union and jobs are sought after in the public schools. It is a particularly challenging job market for elementary, physical education, and social studies teachers. I was looking for a science position. Since the county is growing in the northern/western area, there were possibilities for me to find a job. There are also two fairly urban districts that I did not apply to. I didn't feel that would work for me for my first year.

Tim: *How long were you job searching? How many interviews did you get?*

Wendy: I looked starting in March and was offered a job in late June. I had nine interviews with six districts, including one charter school.

Tim: *Wow. You were invited to lots of interviews! What's your secret to getting these invitations?*

Wendy: At first I just filled out the on-line applications and called Human Resources departments to find out what to do (as the instructions say). Then my business sense (I was in sales eleven years) took over. Why not go right to the person(s) making the decisions? So, I kept records and sent out cover letters and résumés to every principal in my driving area (45 minutes), and a few that were a little farther.

It was 23 districts in four different counties. I also applied to every job on-line that I was qualified for. Since I am certified to teach in a middle school or high school, each principal got a letter, all tailored to the age group and specific school. This takes lots of research on-line, but I think it secured me most of my interviews.

Human Resources always had my application package, or if they did not take applications, I mentioned that my application was on-line at _____ (whichever on-line résumé service they used—there are three main ones around here). I also hand-delivered a few letters. This is a great tactic, and I would have done more of it had I considered it earlier in the hunt.

If I was unfamiliar with a district, I drove there, dressed in interview clothes, and looked around to get a feel for it. I went in, left my résumé, and asked for information on the district. Then I mailed a follow-up letter and résumé.

Tim: *How did you perfect your cover letter and résumé?*

Wendy: My cover letter and résumé had been read over and critiqued by three people, who examined my spelling, grammar, and clarity. I printed it on an off-white paper, but didn't spend a fortune on special envelopes or heavy résumé paper. Most importantly, it brought attention to what I could bring to their school and my most important attributes. In my case, I felt that was my life experiences, my maturity in terms of handling classroom management, and my several certifications that provided the district flexibility in placing me. The cover letter is the first impression the principal will get of a candidate. This needs to be perfect: well thought out, no mistakes, good looking, and names all spelled correctly. A candidate's best attributes should not only highlighted, but given in reference to how they could benefit that school.

Tim: *Were there any interview questions that you were asked at more than one interview? What were they?*

Wendy:

- Greatest strengths/weaknesses
- What did you struggle with during student teaching?
- What would your cooperating teachers say about you?
- What questions do you have for us?
- What is your classroom management plan?
- What will be your policy on homework?
- How will you assess your students?
- How will you include reading/writing in your class?
- How will you handle a student with an IEP?
- How do you motivate students?
- What sports or clubs would you be willing to sponsor?
- How will you differentiate instruction?
- How will you prepare your students for the state tests?
- Tell us about a success you had/a time when you failed.
- Describe a lesson/unit that went well.
- What would we see if we walked in your classroom?

In middle school interviews, there were lots of questions on teaming, middle school philosophy, and integrating other subject areas.

In high school interviews, I noticed that there were more questions on lessons, getting and keeping student interest, preparing for state tests, and questions on content as far as what do students like best.

Tim: *Do you believe in asking questions at the end of your interviews?*

Wendy: Always, always have thoughtful questions to ask at the end. (I think this is incredibly important because it shows your interest in THAT district.)

Some questions I asked were:
- What are you most proud of about your school?
- How many students are there per class?
- What technology and training are available?
- Do the regular education teachers work closely with the special education teachers?
- What mentoring system do you have for first year teachers?

If they brought up anything special about their school, I asked them to elaborate. Always at the end, I would ask what the next step was and when I should hear something.

If you don't ask questions, they may get the impression that you don't care where you work. They'll think you're saying, "Just give me a job," and that you feel their school is interchangeable with others. They know you are looking elsewhere, but try to act as if you have standards and let them know what you like about THEM!

Tim: Do you have advice for people who are qualified candidates, but haven't gotten calls for interviews?

Wendy:

1. Make sure the principal of every school you are interested in has a copy of your résumé, hand-delivered or mailed directly. Human Resources should have your application package.

2. Have others check your cover letter and résumé. Don't be proud. It may make sense to you, but others will be confused at your "point." Ask them to think like a principal. Are you letting the principal know why he/she should consider you? Just because you have the correct certification, or went to school there, or need a job, or did your student teaching there—so what? That wasn't meant meanly, just that the principal is looking for what YOU can bring to his/her school. There will always be some cases where the job is given to someone with connections. Get over it and move on.

3. Apply everywhere in your driving "area." Only you can decide what that is. If you can move, that opens great possibilities. Apply on-line, look in the paper, and talk to people. I also applied to charter schools and private schools. They don't pay as much money, but they do provide experience.

4. If you are in a glutted field, find something to set you apart. Do some volunteer work, start working on another certification, take a job as an aide or a substitute, and express in your cover letter your willingness to be flexible.

5. If what you are doing is not working, you must change tactics! Ask for advice and take some of it. Ask other teachers. Call a local principal and ask for ten minutes of their time. Show them your résumé/ cover letter and ask if they can give you advice.

6. Keep trying, and don't get bitter. No one is "owed" a job because they are qualified. Many people graduate from college and cannot find work in their chosen field right away. Make a contingency plan to get you through. Many people find permanent positions through long-term sub work.

Tim: *Do you have any other interview tips to share?*

Wendy:

1. Show up at least 15 minutes early. I was always there 30 minutes early, but waited in my car until 15 minutes before. Several principals thanked me for coming early.

2. Practice all questions ahead of time. There are plenty of lists of sample interview questions on-line and most list the main questions. Think of examples from your own experience.

3. Know the school so you can tailor the responses. Middle schools are run differently than high schools, so my answers would vary.

4. Better safe than sorry—dress in a suit/dress. Be well groomed and conservative. I saw many casually dressed interviewees and I think this sends a message that you are not taking it seriously. Be very prepared.

5. Bring a portfolio. If they ask about lessons, you can open it and show them. Offer to leave it. If you live close enough, take it a day or two before and leave it for the principal to look through.

6. Be yourself. Don't try to be someone you are not. It will be difficult and you will seem stilted.

7. If they ask a question you are unprepared for, what will you do? I decided ahead to take a deep breath, think for ten seconds or so, and give an honest answer. No sense trying to figure out in ten seconds what you are "supposed" to say. The good interviewers always ask at least one unique question.

8. Go prepared to show you know something about the school and district. Do your homework. Know which clubs/sports you would be willing to help with.

9. Always, always send a thank you note to everyone involved. Hand-deliver it, if possible.

10. Try to have a couple of interviews before any real "dream job" interview. You get much better at it. Apply to schools that need applicants more. You may end up liking them anyway!

Tim: *Do you have any advice for candidates who are stressed out and frustrated with the job search?*

Wendy: Give yourself a day or evening to wallow in self pity. Eat chocolate or ice cream or whatever. Then move on. None of those negative feelings will help.

All job searches are stressful and frustrating. Education is different in its own way, but so are other fields.

Try not to look for someone/something to "blame." In every field, people get jobs because of who they know. A teaching certification doesn't "entitle" you to a job; it just qualifies you to teach. There is a difference, and to have the right attitude to sell yourself, you have to accept that in most cases, they have plenty of other options.

If you feel those with connections are getting the jobs, make connections. Volunteer in the schools. Go to the school board meetings. If you want to work in the district where you pay taxes, even better. Take advantage of the opportunities you have to meet with the district administration as a taxpayer. I served on a strategic planning committee in my home district as a parent representative. I met many administrators.

Don't be shy about asking for advice from other teachers or administrators. Call or e-mail and ask if they will give advice. Most people love to give advice! Be one who asks for it and takes it.

Tim: *How do you feel now that you've gotten a job?*

Wendy: Incredibly relieved and happy. Excited to start and nervous about everything I don't know. Happy I have friends from university who will be starting with me, and appreciating the advice I have been given.

Tim: *Anything else you'd like to say related to teaching, interviewing, or job searching?*

Wendy: Looking for a job is always a full-time job. Do everything you can. Don't stop looking until you have a contract in your hands. Remember you are interviewing them also. Don't work somewhere where you think the principal is a jerk. I have heard some terrible stories, but all my interviews were very professional.

I think the best advice is to be positive. Just as you will stay away from negative teachers when you start, don't pay attention to the whiners and moaners. Everybody gets down sometimes, but you have to get back at it—that's life. Don't think your college is to blame that you paid for an education in an overcrowded field. It's not their job to look into job availability before accepting your money. If you always have a back-up plan, you won't feel desperate!

Wendy, many thanks for taking the time to share your experiences! And congratulations on landing the job!

Wendy is proof-positive that with a little preparation and hard work, you can land a teaching job in even the most competitive areas.

Interview Expert #2:
Rebecca's Experience as a Teacher Interviewer

Next, you'll read a conversation with Rebecca, our second interview expert. She's been teaching in a California elementary school for three years and has recently served on an interview committee that was hiring a 4th grade teacher. Here are some of her thoughts from the *other* side of the interview table:

Tim: *Let's begin with some background information about you and your teaching situation.*

Rebecca: I teach in the state of California in a small town. I currently teach 4th and 5th graders, and their age ranges from 9 to 11 years old. I have been a teacher for three full academic years.

Tim: *Describe the job market for teachers in your area.*

Rebecca: The job market is generally very competitive, but we also have a shortage of teachers in certain subject areas.

Tim: Let's talk about the interview committee you sat in on. You were hiring someone for what position?

Rebecca: *We were hiring someone for a 4th grade position.*

Tim: How many other people were on the committee? Who were they?

Rebecca: There were a total of three teachers. I was the 4/5 teacher and the other two teachers were 5th grade teachers. The principal was also a member of the committee.

Tim: *What are some of the questions that you asked the candidates?*

Rebecca:

- Describe your teaching background.
- What do you think about working on a team?
- How will you address the needs of ELL and special education students?
- What will we see going on inside your classroom?
- What is your policy on classroom discipline?

Tim: *Can you describe a memorable moment at the interview table?*

Rebecca: The one moment that sticks out in my head as memorable is a lady that came in for the interview. She was not very sharply dressed, her hair was a mess, and she had on a shirt that revealed a little too much skin on the upper half of her body.

When she answered the first question, she went on and on for about 15 minutes. We only allotted 30 minutes per interview. She repeated herself a lot throughout the answering process. When answering the questions, she closed her eyes and wouldn't look at anyone.

When asked why she wanted to teach at my school, her answer was not too convincing. She stated that she wanted to teach at my school because she wanted to move out of the greater L.A. area and provide a better place for her child to live. If the lady did her research, she would have known that the school she was at was one of the greatest schools around! We finally had to end the interview, and we did not get to all the questions.

After the interview, all on the committee wanted to bang our heads on the table. It was the worst experience ever.

Tim: *How can you tell if a candidate is a good fit for your school?*

Rebecca: I can tell if a candidate is good for my school when he/she clicks with the people on the panel. The candidate is very professional and understands and answers all the questions correctly. Also, a good candidate is able to bring in their own personal knowledge and experience to the table. A good candidate would be one that has ideas and wants to implement those ideas at my school.

Tim: *What are some of the criteria you used to judge candidates?*

Rebecca: We used a number system. We scored the candidates based on a five-point system and then we added all the numbers up and put the total amount on the back of the paper. The candidates that received the highest numbers were
lumped together. Then we sat around and discussed each of the possible candidates as a group and narrowed it down to two possible people. The principal then checked the references and made his final decision. However, his final

decision was greatly influenced by the teachers' decision as well.

Tim: *Describe a candidate that is well-prepared for an interview.*

Rebecca: Our first impression of a candidate is his/her physical appearance. A candidate that is well-prepared for an interview will be dressed professionally, have hair that is done nicely, and, if female, wears very little makeup. I believe the candidate should opt to wear no perfume (male or female) because many smells can bother the people doing the interview, and this may turn them off.

The candidate will have done his/her research on the school and community. When answering questions the candidate will make eye contact with everyone in the room and answer the question to the best of his/her ability. The candidate will not move around nervously, and their hands will be above the table at all times.

Tim: *Describe a candidate that is poorly prepared for an interview.*

Rebecca: A candidate that is poorly prepared for an interview often lacks a professional appearance. His/her hair will not be neat, they may have strong perfume/cologne on, and [female candidates] may be wearing too much makeup.

Also, a poorly prepared candidate will not have done any research about the school or community. The candidate will not answer the questions being asked correctly, there will be no eye contact, and the candidate will move around a lot in their seat. Also, when answering the questions, the candidate will often say, "ummm" and "ahhhh" or pause a lot. It's easy to tell when a candidate doesn't have enough experience or isn't confident in his/her ability to teach.

Tim: *At the end of an interview, did you give the candidates a chance to ask you questions? If so, what are some of the questions candidates have asked?*

Rebecca: Yes, we gave the candidates a chance to ask questions and even add anything they felt necessary. Some candidates showed off their portfolios, while other candidates tried to show off their knowledge about the community and school.

Tim: *Did the whole group agree on who the best candidate was? Explain.*

Rebecca: The whole group agreed on the top four candidates, and when we narrowed it down to two candidates, the group agreed again. However, at this point one teacher really did not say who she thought was more qualified for the job. The other two teachers felt that one of the candidates was the one that should get the job based on her answers.

Tim: *How can a candidate make their cover letter and résumé appealing to interviewers?*

Rebecca: A candidate should make their cover letter and résumé appealing. First, make sure both are free and clear of typos and errors. Second, make sure that you follow a professional format for the cover letter and résumé. Third, use both high quality paper and type. Lastly, remember to keep it short and to the point.

Tim: *How can a candidate prepare for an interview?*

Rebecca: A candidate can prepare for an interview by doing their research about the school, community, and district. Then the candidate should go around and ask other teachers about the interview process and what to expect. The candidate should also practice answering questions in front of a mirror or with another person. If possible, the candidate should visit the school during a typical school day. The candidate should also try on the clothes a day before the interview and sit down and practice answering interview-type questions.

Tim: *What are your thoughts on teaching portfolios?*

Rebecca: A teaching portfolio can be a good guide to use during the interview. It can reinforce any answers that the person is trying to answer. Overall, the candidate should be proud of using the portfolio and show it off whenever possible.

Tim: *What would you suggest to qualified candidates who have been called in for several interviews at different schools, but haven't gotten a job?*

Rebecca: Keep trying. However, do take a look at how you are dressed and what you are saying at the interview.

Rebecca, many thanks for sharing your experiences and advice with us! It's certainly helpful to know what interviewers are noticing and looking for.

Interview Expert #3:
Lisa's Experiences as a Teacher Interviewer

Finally, I present our third interview expert—Lisa. She served on an interview committee to help her rural school district school find the best candidate for a middle school language arts position. Here's her take on the interview process:

Tim: *Tell us about yourself. What grade and subject do you teach? How long have you been a teacher?*

Lisa: I am certified to teach secondary English. My current assignment is 7th grade reading and language arts. I have completed seven years of teaching.

Tim: *In what state do you live?*

Lisa: I live in Wisconsin and teach in a rural school.

Tim: *Describe the job market for teachers in your area.*

Lisa: The job market for teachers is extremely competitive here (with the exception of secondary math). We have an over-abundance of teachers, and there are several colleges and universities nearby.

Tim: *Let's talk about the last interview committee you served on. You were hiring someone for what position?*

Lisa: We were hiring a 7th grade language arts teacher.

Tim: *How many other people were on the committee? Who were they?*

Lisa: I was an 8th grade language arts teacher when I participated in interviews. Our principal was head of the committee. There were also two other teachers who were members of the 7th grade team.

Tim: *List some questions that you (the committee) asked the candidates.*

Lisa: Some of the questions I remember asking include:
1. Tell us a little bit about who you are.
2. Which five adjectives would you use to describe yourself? Why?
3. How would you describe your teaching style?
4. What do you see as your greatest personal asset that contributes to your teaching style?
5. What is your greatest professional weakness? How do you address this weakness?
6. Which of your teachers left the biggest impression on you as a student, and how has your experience with that teacher shaped the way you teach?
7. What assets will you bring to our students? Team? School? Community?
8. How will you get parents and the community involved in our school?
9. Describe a time you were successful.

10. Tell us about a unit (that you created) with which you are particularly proud.

11. What is a teachable moment? Describe a time you have taken advantage of a teachable moment.

12. How would you explain the "middle school philosophy" to someone who is not familiar with it?

Tim: *Describe a memorable moment at the interview table.*

Lisa: One of the applicants arrived in casual clothing. During the interview, she would only address her answers to the principal. When asked a few of the questions, she kind of dismissed them without giving an answer. It was almost like she didn't think they were worthy of her time. Her attitude at the end of the interview was shocking. It's great when an applicant shows interest by asking questions and leaving with a strong closing statement, but she was quite abrupt and acted as though we had already offered her the job. She even said, "I would like to see my room and my textbooks now. When will I receive a class roster?"

There were also applicants whose outfits were completely inappropriate for the situation, especially among first-time teachers. Some clothes are fashionable but not appropriate for interviews.

Tim: *How can you tell if a candidate is a good fit for your school?*

Lisa: It is difficult to explain what makes a interviewer feel whether or not a candidate is a good fit for the school. It is a good sign when the applicant seems to comfortably participate in the interview. Some people make the interview process seem more like a conversation than a question-and-answer session. It is difficult to hire someone who doesn't seem to be showing his/her true personality in the interview. Getting a handle on an applicant's personality is a combination between his/her mien, responses, and questions. An applicant's teaching style is often a good indicator of how well he/she would fit.

Tim: *What are some of the criteria you used to judge candidates?*

Lisa: We looked at the candidates' confidence levels and the amount of interest they showed in our district. Personality was also very important, so candidates that seemed "at home" during the interview had a strong advantage over other candidates. We also discussed their answers to certain questions.

Tim: Describe a candidate that is well-prepared for an interview.

Lisa: A candidate who is well-prepared arrives a few minutes early wearing an appropriate outfit (a classic look is often better than fashion trends). He or she will have an organized portfolio to share with the committee and be able to effectively use it to support his/her answers. One candidate had a large portfolio in a binder, but she also brought an abridged folder for each member on the panel. She also left one of these folders for us to refer to after the interview.

It is also impressive when the candidate has some knowledge of the district and/or community. Candidates who ask good questions about the district, staff, and school philosophy seem very well-prepared.

A well-prepared candidate is confident while answering questions. He or she listens to the questions, takes a moment to collect his/her thoughts, and then answers the question thoroughly.

Tim: *Describe a candidate that is poorly prepared for an interview.*

Lisa: Candidates who do not bring work samples or who dress inappropriately are generally not well-prepared. Applicants do not seem well-prepared if they consistently find it difficult to answer questions or flounder through answers, seeming to make things up as he/she goes along.

Tim: *What are some of the questions candidates have asked?*

Lisa:

- What aspects of the middle school philosophy are a strong presence in your school?
- What extracurricular activities and duties are available for me?
- What is the school climate like?
- How does the community view the school or education in general?
- What are some goals the district (or building) has for improvement?
- What does the district do to teach students important lessons that stretch beyond academic disciplines?

Tim: *Did the whole group agree on who the best candidate was?*

Lisa: We began by narrowing the field. If anyone on the committee had an extreme distaste for any of the applicants, that applicant was removed from the pool. Once we had a smaller pool, we began talking about each of the candidates. The content-area folks weighed in with their thoughts about teaching style, while the grade-level teachers focused on traits that would make each candidate an asset to the team and projects that extend beyond content area.

Tim: *How can a candidate make their résumé appealing to interviewers?*

Lisa: Résumés with concisely-written bullets are very user-friendly, especially during the interview. It is not necessary to list every duty performed at previous jobs. For non-teaching jobs, only include duties that demonstrate an asset relevant to your teaching career. For teaching jobs, do not include things that every teacher does (like write lesson plans or attend staff meetings).

Tim: *How can a candidate prepare for an interview?*

Lisa: Get your hands on any type of interview questions you can find and work on coming up with answers. If you can find an item to include in your portfolio that will support what you are saying, include it. Then practice, practice, practice! Find someone who will go through interview questions with you so you can practice answering questions while using your portfolio.

Tim: *What are your thoughts on teaching portfolios?*

Lisa: Portfolios are great, but only when the candidate knows how to use them. Don't just give it to the panel to have them flip through it. Frankly, there isn't time to really look at the portfolios, and no one wants to sift through them on their own. Use it throughout the entire interview to show examples that support what you are saying.

Tim: *What would you suggest to qualified candidates who have been called in for several interviews at different schools, but haven't gotten a job?*

Lisa: Do some research about the school and community. Try to find something that will give you an edge over people who are not familiar with the school and/or community.

If you know people from the school or community, talk to them. It will give you some ideas for the school and community climate, and networking can be your greatest asset.

Sit back and evaluate the interviews that you have been on. What went well for you? Where do you have room for improvement? Get some feedback: go over some of your responses with other people in the educational field.

Tim: *What would you suggest to candidates who are qualified, but have not been invited to interviews?*

Lisa: Work on strengthening your résumé and cover letter. If you know anything about the community or school, try to incorporate that into the first or final paragraph of your letter. It will make your letter stand out among the flood of letters that districts must sift through. Also be sure to proofread carefully. Many districts will throw out a letter or résumé because there is one mistake, however little it may be. Look at your résumé to see if there are things that you could do to make it more "user-friendly." Have you been concise? Is it easy for interviewers to quickly look at your résumé and find specific items?

Lisa, I would like to extend a huge thank you for sharing this information with us! You've offered sound and practical advice that candidates can use!

Good Luck!

I hope you found this guide helpful. Good luck to you in all your future endeavors.

- Tim Wei

Contact Me

I'd love to hear from you! Questions, feedback, and ideas are all welcome. I enjoy reading and responding to your thoughts on this book. Unlike many other more prolific (and wealthier) authors, I usually have time to respond to your questions and comments personally. My e-mail address is:

tim@iwantateachingjob.com

I hope you'll consider writing me if:

1. You get a job (There's nothing I enjoy more than e-mail messages with the title, "I got a job!")

2. Something in this book helped you

3. You've come across a tough interview question and don't know how to tackle it (Maybe I can help!)

4. You have a suggestion that will help me improve the next version of this book (I'm always looking to make this book bigger and better.)

5. You just want to chat about your job-hunting experiences

Thank You

Many people have helped make this book possible.

Thanks to **Cynthia Sherwood** for editing the book. Without her perfectionism, careful eye, and way-with-words, the content of this book wouldn't be nearly as clear as it is now.

Muchas gracias to **Wendy**, **Rebecca**, and **Lisa** for their interviews. I really appreciate them taking the time to share their experiences and for letting me publish them!

I appreciate **Robin**'s help by sharing her cover letter and résumé expertise with me.

Thanks to **my wife** for her patience and for letting me use the computer all the time. :)

And, of course, the biggest thanks of all goes to **you** for purchasing the book. Your support and positive feedback are what really makes it worthwhile. I hope you found it to be a helpful and informative resource. Best of luck on your job search!

Made in the USA
Lexington, KY
15 May 2014